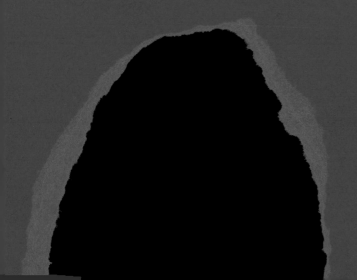

Gallery Books
Editor: Peter Fallon

THE SALVAGE SHOP

Jim Nolan

THE SALVAGE SHOP

Gallery Books

The Salvage Shop
is first published
simultaneously in paperback
and in a clothbound edition
on 13 October 1998.

The Gallery Press
Loughcrew
Oldcastle
County Meath
Ireland

ISBN 1 85235 228 0 (*paperback*)
       1 85235 229 9 (*clothbound*)

The Gallery Press acknowledges the financial assistance of An Chomhairle Ealaíon / The Arts Council, Ireland, and the Arts Council of Northern Ireland.

Characters

SYLVIE TANSEY
EDDIE TANSEY, *Sylvie's son*
KATIE TANSEY, *Eddie's daughter*
RITA SHANAHAN
STEPHEN KEARNEY
JOSIE COSTELLO

Time and place

Summer. The present. The Salvage Shop in Garris, a small coastland town.

The Salvage Shop was first produced by Red Kettle Theatre Company at the Garter Lane Theatre, Waterford, on Monday, 19 January 1998, with the following cast:

EDDIE TANSEY	John Olohan
SYLVIE TANSEY	Niall Toibín
STEPHEN KEARNEY	Ray McBride
KATIE TANSEY	Emily Nagle
RITA SHANAHAN	Caroline Gray
JOSIE COSTELLO	David Heap

Director	Ben Barnes
Set Design	Ben Hennessy
Lighting Design	Nick McCall
Assisted by	Jim Daly
Costume Design	Mona Manahan
Musical Advisor	Liam Walsh

The Dublin Theatre Festival production, in association with Noel Pearson and Gaiety Stage Productions, opened at The Gaiety Theatre, Dublin, on Tuesday, 13 October 1998.

In memory of my father
John Nolan

ACT ONE

Scene One

The Salvage Shop. Early summer. Night. As lights come up, we find
EDDIE *alone in the shop, working on a piece of furniture at the carpentry desk. From the upstairs bedroom we hear the aria 'A teo o cara' from Bellini's* I Puritani, *sung by Luciano Pavarotti. We hold this for a moment or two. Then, offstage, we hear a car engine approaching and pulling up. As the car door opens and we hear voices off,* EDDIE *goes upstairs, turns off stereo and, returning, checks the contents of a saucepan on the cooking ring in the kitchen area before returning to desk.*

STEPHEN (*Offstage*) Out you come, Sylvie. Home, sweet home!

SYLVIE (*Offstage. Getting out of car. Obviously drunk*) Home sweet fucking home is right, Stephen! We thank thee, O'Reilly, for these, thy lifts, which of thy bounty we have just received —

STEPHEN That's enough now, Sylvie — you'll wake poor Eddie.

SYLVIE Fuck poor Eddie and all who sail in him. And fuck you too, Reilly! Take the sanctimonious sneer off yer gob — ye're ugly enough the way God made you.

STEPHEN Now, Sylvie, there's no call for —

SYLVIE There is a call, Stephen, and Master Reilly here would do well to remember it. Bandroom, eight o'clock tomorrow night. Captain Tansey back at the helm, mutiny quelled, order restored. Do you receive my meaning, Master Reilly? (*We hear car engine screeching away*) We'll take that as a yes. Let us proceed, Stephen — into the citadel!

The doors crash open and SYLVIE *rolls in, supported*

with some difficulty by STEPHEN. EDDIE *barely acknowledges them.*

STEPHEN *(As they enter)* Ah — Eddie — the mercy of God, you're still up. I'd never have managed him on them stairs.

SYLVIE *(Goes directly to desk in 'office' area)* The mercy of God has nothing to do with it, Stephen — Eddie here is still up because he has nothing better to do. Isn't that right, Eddie? And as for the stairs, Tansey will tackle them in his own time. *(Pause)* By Jesus, when I think of it!

STEPHEN *(Apprehensive)* What's that, Sylvie?

SYLVIE You know bloody well what's that! And you a party to it.

Takes whiskey bottle and glass from drawer, noticing someone's been drinking it, glares at EDDIE *who sets knife and fork etc at the office desk, where* SYLVIE *now sits.*

STEPHEN I never laid a hand on ye, Sylvie. As God is my judge, I didn't.

SYLVIE *(Mimicking* STEPHEN*)* 'As God is my judge I didn't.' *(Bellows)* By your silence you condone them, Mr Kearney! Manhandled out of my own bandroom, frog-marched into the street for the town to sneer at and fecked in to the back of a car like a sack of old spuds. And to bate it all, whose car is it, only Reilly's!

STEPHEN Decent enough of him, after all was said, Sylvie.

SYLVIE Is it risin' me you are! What bejaysus chance have I when me own are crossin' the floor to the enemy's ranks?

STEPHEN I'm only sayin', Sylvie.

SYLVIE Betrayal, Mr Kearney, is what that amounts to. *(Looking at* EDDIE*)* And a long and honourable tradition of that commodity in this shop, if anyone needs reminding. But Tansey won't be bested. *(Drinks)*

Drunk and incapable, says Reilly. Come back when you're sober, says Reilly. And tell me now, Master Reilly, says I, what fool could stand sober in front of this half-arsed excuse for a band?

STEPHEN We do our best.

SYLVIE Your best is not bloody well good enough. Three days to a two-bit competition in Ballin-fucking-collig and you turn the screw on your conductor — don't tell me you're doing your best.

> *Throughout the foregoing, from* SYLVIE *and* STEPHEN's *entrance,* EDDIE *has been preparing food for* SYLVIE. *Through* SYLVIE's *tirade, he remains impassive and his movement in setting up the table, laying it, preparing and serving food, should have about it all the appearance of tried and tested routine. He puts the plate in front of* SYLVIE *right on cue.*

EDDIE You've said your piece — now eat.

> *Silence.* SYLVIE, *who has been carried on the wave of his oratory, is briefly stilled by* EDDIE's *intervention. Pauses. Looks at food. Looks contemptuously at* EDDIE, *looks back to food before scattering it violently from the table.*

SYLVIE (*As he does*) Eat my bollox!

> *Silence.* SYLVIE *at the table, head lowered.* EDDIE *watching him,* STEPHEN *shocked and embarrassed. After a moment or two* EDDIE *breaks away, begins to hum a tune as he picks up food and plate from floor and puts them in rubbish bin.* SYLVIE *doesn't move.*

STEPHEN If I may say so, Sylvie — that's a bit much.

SYLVIE No, you may not say so, Mr Kearney. Not in my shop, not under my roof. And if you don't like it, you can take yourself, your lame duck instrument and your creeping Jesus glass and get the fuck out of my house.

EDDIE You'd better go, Stephen.

STEPHEN *(Pause)* Goodnight, Eddie.

STEPHEN *exits,* EDDIE *sees him out, closes door. Silence.*

SYLVIE Don't you judge me. *(Pause)* You have no right to judge me.

EDDIE No, I don't. You can do that all by yourself tomorrow.

SYLVIE Not fit. Any of yous. To lick my fucking boots.

EDDIE That's right, Sylvie — not a one. Now give me the bottle — you've had your fill for one day.

SYLVIE I've had my fill alright — of Master Reilly and his cohorts. Mediocrities, the whole damned lot of them.

EDDIE Give me the bottle, Sylvie.

SYLVIE When it's good and empty. And I'll go when I'm good and ready. But not *pushed*, Eddie. There's a move on, y'know. And that bollox Reilly is behind it. He can see his grubby hand on the baton and he won't let go. 'Word on the ground is we're going to lose the Regatta job again next month,' says he. 'That's three years runnin' the Strand Road band'll have it. Not to mention Corpus Christi last week. Begod but you have to hand it to the Strand Road lads,' says he — in his element now and his sidekicks lappin' it up. 'Didn't they look well in their shiny new uniforms at the head of the procession. Question is,' says he, 'what are we going to do about it?' That was last night's episode. I looked around the room, and dared them one by one to cast the first stone. *(Pause)* Silence, Eddie. 'Well,' says I, 'if no one else has anything to contribute we shall proceed with our rehearsal.'

EDDIE Game, set and match to Tansey.

SYLVIE Bloody sure of it.

EDDIE It's a pity you were drunk tonight.

SYLVIE It's *why* I was drunk tonight. (*Pause*) They don't trust me anymore. Not just Reilly and his like but the old guard as well.

EDDIE You should go, so.

SYLVIE Like you did! No, not like that. And not like this either. Head high and in my own time. (*Drinks*) And Ballin-fucking-collig is only the first instalment. Not exactly the National Championships, I grant you, but it's a start. The Strand Road boys are travelling too, I hear, but it'll take more than a shiny new uniform to best Tansey. And when we win I'll shove that cup so far up Reilly's hole, he'll be shittin' silver for a month.

EDDIE Good on ye, Sylvie.

SYLVIE Don't patronise me. They're right. I should have stepped down years ago. And would have. Until you walked into the sunset.

EDDIE (*Sings quietly but with insistence*) 'The Minstrel Boy to the war has gone — '

SYLVIE Sneer if you like, Eddie, but it's the truth and you know it.

EDDIE That's an old record now, Sylvie.

SYLVIE No. This was my legacy, boy. This mess was what you left me when you walked.

EDDIE And you'll never tire of reminding me. But it happened. Leave it alone now.

SYLVIE I can't leave it alone. The consequences, see. Passing the baton. My father's hand to mine, my hand to yours. That's how it was meant to be, Eddie.

EDDIE If it hurts that much, let it go.

SYLVIE No. Because I'm not like you. I don't run for shelter at the first sign of rain.

EDDIE It was a bit more than a drop of rain. (*Pause*) C'mon. I'll give you a hand with the stairs.

SYLVIE That won't be necessary.

EDDIE I'd like to.

SYLVIE I can manage on my own.

EDDIE Fair enough.

SYLVIE What are you doing here anyway?

EDDIE   I worked back for a bit. This table needs finishing by Saturday.

SYLVIE   Back *here*, I mean. Under *my* roof. Is the penthouse suite over the Amusement Arcade not to your taste anymore? Or did lovely Rita give you the chop?

EDDIE   I thought you'd be glad of the company.

SYLVIE   I don't need company.

EDDIE   I was joking, Sylvie — this is just temporary.

SYLVIE   (*Silence*) Aye. Well, see you remember that.

EDDIE   I will. (*As* SYLVIE *goes upstairs*) You'll eat tomorrow, won't you, Sylvie?

SYLVIE   I'll eat when I'm hungry.

EDDIE   You're not well. You have to eat.

SYLVIE   I don't need a nursemaid. If that's what you're here for, you can fuck back to yer Amusement Hall.

EDDIE   (*To himself*)That's not why I'm here.

> SYLVIE *enters bedroom and sits on bed, unlacing boots.* EDDIE *resumes work as, after a moment or two,* KATIE *enters, carrying rucksack, hold-all etc.*

KATIE   I know, I know! Don't say a word. I know I'm late and there's no excuse for it and I'm always the same and I never really loved you anyway. I know all that, so don't say a word! (*Pause*) Howya, Da — long time no see.

EDDIE   (*With a touch of sarcasm*) A pleasure deferred is a pleasure enhanced. (*Kisses her*) You should have called, Katie.

KATIE   I know. I'm sorry. A few of us went for a beer after the last exam. You can guess the rest.

EDDIE   I'd rather not.

KATIE   (*As, upstairs,* SYLVIE *goes to stereo and turns on CD*) Might be as well. Anyway, better late than never. And before you ask, I *did* sit every paper and I answered *all* the questions and I kept writing to the last bell *just* like you told me. So if they *do* fire me out, it won't be for the want of bullshit.

EDDIE   We can ask no more!

KATIE (*We hear the music from Sylvie's room, 'Amor ti vieta' from Giordano's* Fedora) That's a bad sign.

EDDIE His comfort blanket.

KATIE I heard about the row with Reilly.

EDDIE Bush telegraph out already, is it?

KATIE Tommy Mullins that plays the cornet was above at the station. He gave me a blow by blow account.

EDDIE I'm sure he did.

KATIE Is he taking it bad?

EDDIE You know Sylvie — he's thriving on it.

KATIE I'll run up and say hello.

EDDIE I wouldn't, Kate.

KATIE Why not? — I haven't seen him since Easter.

EDDIE He's tired and emotional, that's why.

KATIE (*Smiles*) Pissed, y'mean.

EDDIE You can see him tomorrow.

KATIE Yes Daddio! What has you here so late anyway? I had to lug this stuff all the way up to the flat — I'll have a hump on me back tomorrow with the weight of the rucksack.

EDDIE You'll survive. I was working back. You know me — nothing better to do!

KATIE There's plenty you could be doing if you put your mind to it. Speaking of which, how's Rita? I called in just now but there was no one there, either.

EDDIE Rita's fine.

KATIE You don't sound too convinced.

EDDIE I haven't seen her for a while.

KATIE Lovers' tiff?

EDDIE We're not lovers, Katie.

KATIE That's right, I forgot. You just sleep in each other's beds every now and then. Hardly qualifies, does it?

EDDIE That's enough, Katie.

KATIE (*Lightly*) She's too bloody good for you anyway.

EDDIE Undoubtedly. (*Pause*) I've moved back here for a while.

KATIE What's wrong?

EDDIE Nothing's wrong. Change of scenery, that's all.

KATIE What's wrong, Da?

EDDIE Nothing! Sylvie's getting on a bit. If I stay here it's easier to keep an eye on him.

KATIE I'm sure he's enjoying that!

EDDIE You can imagine.

KATIE Rita must be disappointed.

EDDIE Rita's my landlady, not my keeper, Katie.

KATIE Go on! You're practically living together.

EDDIE (*With infinite patience*) I rent rooms over the Amusement Arcade. She has her place, I have mine. That hardly constitutes living together.

KATIE I stand corrected, Papa! How can you ever forgive me!

EDDIE With great difficulty. Anyway, this is just temporary. I've left a month's rent with Rita, so you can park your ass up there for the summer.

KATIE (*Pause. Uncertain*) I have some news too, Da.

EDDIE (*An anxious glance at her stomach*) What kind of news?

KATIE Not that kind, you idiot. I don't *do* babies.

EDDIE Delighted to hear it.

KATIE Not yet anyway! (*Pause*) I got a job.

EDDIE My bank manager will be deeply moved.

KATIE (*Pause*) In Costello's Hotel.

Silence. EDDIE *shocked.*

Mags rang last week — said he was advertising. She's there full-time now, y'know.

EDDIE That so?

KATIE Yeah. Anyway, I rang Costello. He's offered me a job in the bar for the summer.

EDDIE How very sweet of him.

KATIE I need the money, Da.

EDDIE Is mine not good enough?

KATIE You know what I mean.

EDDIE I know what Costello means.

KATIE If you'd prefer I didn't —

EDDIE You do as you see fit, Kate.

KATIE What happened with Costello was a long time ago,

Da. Twelve years, to be precise.

EDDIE   I've a long memory.

KATIE   Maybe too long.

EDDIE   You think so.

Silence.

KATIE   (*Gathering bags*) I have to go.

EDDIE   You've only just arrived.

KATIE   I told Mags I'd call in. She's working tonight.

EDDIE   I see. D'you want a lift?

KATIE   No. I'll walk.

EDDIE   I'll drop your bags to the flat.

KATIE   It's all right — I can manage.

EDDIE   Story of the night, it seems. You'll need a key.

KATIE   (*Taking key*) Tell Sylvie I'll see him tomorrow.

EDDIE   Sure.

KATIE   Is he all right, Da?

EDDIE   He's fine. (*Now we hear 'Una furtiva lagrima' from Donizetti's L'Elisir d'Amore*) Mr Pavarotti always does the trick.

KATIE   Still besotted, is he?

EDDIE   (*Nods*) 'Una Furtiva Lagrima' — it's his favourite aria. He told me once he used to play it for your grandmother. Not Pavarotti, of course — Tito Schipa or one of them boys. In his cups sometimes, the long evenings by the fire, he'd play her that song. This is for you, he'd say, this is for you. And she'd know, Katie, she'd know the music was speaking for him. (*Pause*) I must try it myself sometime.

A moment between them. Then KATIE *nods, turns and leaves.* EDDIE *watches her go, listens a moment, turns out lights downstairs and goes out to parlour area as music soars and scene ends.*

Scene Two

The same. Early afternoon the following day. Lights up on empty stage. After a moment or two, RITA enters.

RITA Anybody home? (*Goes to parlour area. Looks out*) Hello? (*Pause*) All quiet on the Western Front.

She drops bag she is carrying and wanders absently through the bric-à-brac and furniture. KATIE enters.

Katie! Katie Tansey! Welcome home!

They rush to each other and embrace.

KATIE Howya, Rita?

RITA All the better for seeing you. When did you get back?

KATIE Last night. Are you on your own?

RITA I was looking for Eddie.

KATIE Must be out to lunch.

RITA Pretty much a permanent condition for your Dad, these days. Well, what news from the capital? How'd the exams go?

KATIE They went.

RITA Best place for them. What about the new boyfriend?

KATIE He went as well.

RITA Same rule applies. Love 'em and leave 'em. Isn't that right, Katie? Tell you what, as I'm not getting any better offers, why don't you and me jump on a bus to Kilmore tonight and have ourselves a feckin' party?

KATIE I can't, Rita.

RITA Why not? My treat. I could do with a bit of a lift.

KATIE I'd love to, Rita — but I'm working.

RITA You never did a day's work in your life, Katie Tansey.

KATIE There's a first time for everything. Look! (*Opens*

jacket to reveal standard-issue white blouse and black skirt) Hardly my style, is it?

RITA Miracles *do* happen!

KATIE D'you recognise it?

RITA No.

KATIE But then you were never a regular in Costello's, were you?

Silence.

RITA Does your Dad know?

KATIE I told him last night. (*Pause*) It's just a job, Rita. You'd think I'd put a knife in his back or something.

RITA You know why.

KATIE I don't care why. Doesn't anybody ever move on in this town?

RITA Not in a hurry, no.

KATIE It's the same between him and Sylvie. It's as if they're all locked in some sort of a bloody time warp. Well I'm not, Rita. It's just a job — and I'm glad of it.

RITA Good for you.

Pause.

KATIE I'm sorry. God knows, you've paid your own price.

RITA If you're talking about me and your Dad, I didn't pay any price I didn't want to. I know his story.

KATIE Some story.

RITA That's as may be, but it's *his* and if it's ever going to change, it's only he can do it.

KATIE Don't you ever wish he would?

RITA *That's* another story.

KATIE He told me he'd moved out. Did yous have a row?

RITA (*Laughs*) Jesus, no! Eddie and me never quite reached that level of engagement.

KATIE What's he up to?

RITA Search me. All I got was a month's rent and a note saying he'd be in touch. That was two weeks ago.

21

KATIE   You were too bloody good for him, Rita. I told him that last night and I meant it.

RITA   (*Smiling*) I'm sure you did but it isn't true. He does have his good points, Katie.

KATIE   (*Lightly*) Name one!

RITA   (*Laughs*) Leave it with me — I'll think of something. (*Pause*) Anyway, at least *you're* back — half a Tansey is better than nothing.

KATIE   There's staff quarters at the hotel. I've decided to stay there for the summer.

RITA   D'you think that's such a good idea?

KATIE   Maybe. Maybe not. But it's what I want. Mags says the crack is mighty.

RITA   I can imagine what Mags says. You'd want to be careful with that one, Katie.

KATIE   Yes, Mammy! (*Pause*) I haven't told *him* yet, Rita.

RITA   My lips are sealed! Bad enough to be working for the devil without sleeping in his den.

> EDDIE *enters, somewhat taken aback to see he has visitors. Notices* KATIE's *uniform.*

EDDIE   Hello, Katie. Rita. How are ye?

RITA   Sunny side up, Eddie! And no use complainin' either — (*Winks at* KATIE) for who'd listen?

EDDIE   Is Sylvie up?

KATIE   Think so. I heard something stirring in the bathroom.

EDDIE   Washing his sins away, I suppose.

KATIE   Very likely.

EDDIE   (*Sets to work at carpentry bench*) You'll have to excuse me — we're fierce busy.

RITA   Is that the way?

EDDIE   It is.

RITA   Well, don't let us interrupt. There's nothing I like more than to watch a skilled craftsman at work. (*To* KATIE) Especially when he's under pressure.

KATIE   (*Making herself scarce*) Merciful God, is that the time?

RITA   What's your hurry, child? You're only in the door.

KATIE Love 'em and leave 'em — isn't that what ye said, Rita? (*Pause*) I started work today, Da.

EDDIE So I notice.

KATIE (*Uniform*) It's shite, isn't it?

EDDIE Yeah. It is.

KATIE (*Pause*) I'll see you around, Rita.

RITA You will, Katie.

KATIE *exits.*

Don't go so hard on her, Eddie. She's not to blame.

EDDIE What d'you want me to do — send the bastard a thank you card? (*Pause*) She's made her choice — it's none of my business.

RITA And none of mine either. (*Produces a bottle of wine from bag*) Here, this might cheer you up. It's not exactly a vintage year but then neither was I.

EDDIE Your birthday. I'm sorry, Rita — I forgot.

RITA So I noticed. Well if Mohammed won't go to the mountain — (*Pops cork, pours drink, raises glass*) Here's mud in your eye, Eddie!

EDDIE (*They drink*) Happy birthday, Rita. I'll make it up to you, I promise.

RITA Yeah. And pigs will fly.

EDDIE No, I'm serious. Saturday night. We'll drive to Kilmore, have a bite to eat, a few drinks — just the two of us.

RITA Yeah. (*Pause*) So, how have you been?

EDDIE All right, and you?

RITA Surviving. Am I allowed to say I miss you?

EDDIE I miss you, too. (*Pause*) Sylvie is dying, Rita.

RITA What?

EDDIE He went back to hospital last month. They called me a fortnight ago.

RITA And?

EDDIE He's dying. Three to six months.

RITA Does he know?

EDDIE Nobody's told him, if that's what you mean, but he's no fool.

RITA I'm sorry, Eddie.

EDDIE Yeah. So am I. I don't know what to do, Rita.

RITA There's limits. You do what you can, that's all.

They hear SYLVIE *beginning to descend stairs.* EDDIE *abruptly changes the subject, leading* RITA *quickly to a piece of furniture draped in a red cloth.*

EDDIE It's called the lovers' seat. Six weeks ago the beam I cut it from, one-hundred-year-old pitch pine, was lying idle on a building site in Manchester. But *salvaged*, Rita. Here, try it for size! (*As* SYLVIE *reaches the foot of the stairs*) Afternoon, Sylvester!

SYLVIE Hello, Rita.

RITA Hello, Mr Tansey.

EDDIE (*Gesturing to seat*) What d'y' think?

SYLVIE (*Goes to desk, takes whiskey from drawer*) 'Twill never take.

EDDIE I cut it off one of the Manchester beams. Came up well, didn't it?

SYLVIE 'Twill never take, I said.

EDDIE You'd never know. There's always a fool somewhere.

SYLVIE (*To* RITA) More in his line, sticking to tables and chairs. Stuff there's call for.

EDDIE Yes. I'll remember that. (*Returns to carpentry desk as* SYLVIE *drinks whiskey. It sits hard on his stomach*) Where are you off to?

SYLVIE My 'constitutional'. Sea air and salt water — if that's all right with you.

EDDIE I'll throw on something before you go. A few spuds maybe — it won't take long.

SYLVIE (*To* RITA) In the name of Jaysus, is it some sort of a fetish he has? I have all the nourishment I need in this.

EDDIE *You have to eat, Sylvie!*

SYLVIE *No!* I do not have to eat. I have to do exactly what I want to do and if you don't like it you can walk out that door. It's no wonder you threw him out, Rita.

RITA   I didn't, Mr Tansey. He went all by himself. (*Pause*)
I'll leave yous to it.

A nod to EDDIE *and* RITA *goes.*

EDDIE   You're a sick man. If you don't eat you'll die.
SYLVIE   And if I do I won't?
EDDIE   (*As* SYLVIE *swallows more whiskey*) Reilly won't wear
that stuff again tonight.
SYLVIE   Hair of the dog, that's all. I'll not give those fuckers
any excuse. If we go down tomorrow night they
won't have Sylvie here as the fall guy.
EDDIE   I hope not.
SYLVIE   Do you? (*Pause*) Well, wait and see, Eddie.

STEPHEN *enters. The events of the previous night
hover over the moment.*

STEPHEN   (*Tentatively*) How's the men?
EDDIE   (*Looks at* SYLVIE, *whose head is low*) The men is fine,
Stephen.

*Takes off jacket, hangs it up and goes to stained glass
section of the shed. He will work throughout the
following sequence.* EDDIE *resumes work also,* SYLVIE
goes towards door.

STEPHEN   Are you headin' out, Sylvie?
SYLVIE   (*As he goes*) Yes, my perambulations. (*Hesitates. Turns*)
I believe I owe you an apology, Stephen.
STEPHEN   For what?
SYLVIE   You know bloody well for what. (*Pause*) I was out of
order. (*This doesn't come easily*) I'm sorry.
STEPHEN   Say no more, Sylvie — we'll forget about it now.
SYLVIE   I'll see you tonight, so. Eight o'clock sharp!
STEPHEN   Please God.
SYLVIE   Yes. You have to believe in something, don't you.
Even if it's only a silver cup in Ballincollig.

SYLVIE *exits.*

EDDIE Is he beyond redemption, Stephen?

STEPHEN (*Smiling*) Nothing is beyond redemption — you know that. The kink is everything, Eddie. When my grandfather made the original windows for the church below, they say he left a flaw in every panel the way the people would remember they were the work of human hands. The mark of Cain he called it.

EDDIE Your grandfather must have been a wise man.

STEPHEN Aye. I suppose he was. (*Pause*) It's not looking good for Sylvie, Eddie.

EDDIE How d'you mean?

STEPHEN There's moves afoot.

EDDIE There's always moves afoot. You'd see more politics in that bandroom than above in the Dáil.

STEPHEN They're going to shaft him, Eddie.

EDDIE They can't shaft him. Reilly doesn't own the band.

STEPHEN Sylvie doesn't either. (*Pause*) I'm sorry, Eddie. But that's what they're saying. And it's not just Reilly and his clique. Some of the older lads have been swayed. They say they'll not play tomorrow if Sylvie's on the baton.

EDDIE That's just talk.

STEPHEN We're on the edge already — two or three more defectors and we could go under altogether.

EDDIE That won't happen — Sylvie'll pull 'em in line.

STEPHEN It's already happening. Reilly's called a meeting in Costello's before the rehearsal tonight. Either Sylvie goes or the band pulls out of the competition.

EDDIE They can't do that.

STEPHEN They're putting it to a vote. Reilly or Sylvie. And if he loses and won't step down, the band doesn't travel.

EDDIE I see.

STEPHEN Reilly was waiting for me when I got home last night. I gave an hour trying to persuade him to hold his fire but the fecker wouldn't budge. They're all of one mind, Eddie.

EDDIE Tansey must go.

STEPHEN Tansey should have gone years ago. But not this way.

EDDIE You know why he didn't.

STEPHEN Don't, Eddie. You had your troubles. I know nothing about such things. Never had a girl in my life, let alone one'd be fool enough to marry me. What you did was one thing and how he took it was another — don't ask me to judge it.

EDDIE (*Pause*) I'll talk to Reilly.

STEPHEN Save your breath — Reilly has even less time for you than for your father.

EDDIE What about the senior lads? Would they listen to me?

STEPHEN They have long memories, Eddie.

EDDIE (*Pause*) Okay. If they want their pound of flesh, let them have it. You go to the meeting, Stephen. Tell them you've spoken to Sylvie and that he's agreed to step down. But not before Saturday.

STEPHEN I can't do that — Sylvie'd crucify me.

EDDIE I'll handle Sylvie. We'll leave it a week or so, make it look like his own decision. And if the band wins the competition, he can go with his head high.

STEPHEN They won't buy it, Eddie — Reilly won't let him off the hook now he can see him wriggling.

EDDIE Say nothing to Reilly. Go to the men directly. They trust you, Stephen.

STEPHEN So does Sylvie — this is like signing his death warrant.

EDDIE At least he won't be kicked out the door.

STEPHEN (*Pause*) I'll see what I can do. No promises, mind, but I'll try.

EDDIE Thanks, Stephen. As you said, nothing is beyond redemption.

EDDIE *and* STEPHEN *resume their separate work as music comes in and lights fade to indicate end of scene.*

Scene Three

The same. Ten o'clock that evening. EDDIE *alone. From Sylvie's room we hear Mozart's* Idomeneo. *As lights come up,* EDDIE *emerges from kitchen area with teapot and cup as* KATIE *enters.*

EDDIE   Buona sera, Signorina Tansey.

KATIE   Buona sera, Papa.

EDDIE   Compositore?

KATIE   Mozart?

EDDIE   Si! E tenore?

KATIE   Pavarotti, of course.

EDDIE   Si. E finalmente — Name that opera!

KATIE   You have me there, Da.

EDDIE   *Idomeneo, King of Crete,* y'eejit!

KATIE   'Twas on the tip of my tongue. Is His Majesty above?

EDDIE   Not yet. I only play them when he's out.

KATIE   Dead right. Be awful if he thought you had something in common.

EDDIE   No fear of that.

KATIE   Do you miss it?

EDDIE   What?

KATIE   Music? The band?

EDDIE   Fond memory brings the light! But, as you said, that was a long time ago.

KATIE   You could have gone back.

EDDIE   D'you think so? (*Pours tea*) Hard day at the office?

KATIE   Don't start, Da.

EDDIE   Paternal concern, that's all. How's the bould Josie, anyway?

KATIE   Please, Da.

EDDIE   God, but you must have raised a few eyebrows though.

KATIE   Do you think I care?

EDDIE   I do!

KATIE   Then you deal with it.

EDDIE   I'm sorry! Takes a bit of getting used to, that's all.

KATIE She was my mother, y'know.

EDDIE I'm sorry!

Pause.

KATIE Do you work this late every night?

EDDIE A little behind in the orders — as the butcher said when he caught his arse in the mincer.

KATIE That's not why you moved back here though, is it?

EDDIE No. Not exactly.

KATIE Sylvie's sick again, isn't he?

EDDIE He's seventy-two, Katie — it's no more than that. The old bugger'll probably see us all out in the end.

KATIE Don't do this, Da. I have a right to know.

EDDIE Yes. You do.

KATIE How bad is it?

EDDIE As bad as it gets.

Silence.

KATIE Does he know?

EDDIE I'm not sure. I think so.

KATIE The band had a meeting in the hotel earlier. Is that why he wasn't there?

EDDIE Reilly's trying to shaft him. Did you hear anything?

KATIE No. Tried to, but the doors were locked.

EDDIE Bastards. That band is all he has left.

KATIE He has you, hasn't he?

EDDIE (*Without conviction*) Yes. He has me.

KATIE I'll help you, Da. Whatever it takes. I'll help you.

EDDIE This isn't your mess, Katie. You know the story on Sylvie and me.

KATIE Yeah. Chapter and verse. But it's not over yet.

SYLVIE *and* STEPHEN *enter,* SYLVIE *singing.*

SYLVIE 'Oh we bet the rest of the Empire's best,
Shur they're only a bunch of queers,
The Munsters have more hair on the chests

Than the British Grenadiers!'

(*To* STEPHEN) *Idomeneo*, Stephen! Idomeneo, King of Crete, returning from the wars at Troy encounters a storm at sea. In order to assuage the elements, the King vows to the Sea God a sacrifice of the first living thing he meets on shore! (*A glance to* EDDIE) Unfortunately for the King, it happened to be his son.

KATIE Howya, Sylvie?

SYLVIE Katie Tansey! How are ye? Give yer old grandad a celebratory kiss.

KATIE (*Kisses him*) What are ye celebrating?

SYLVIE Victory, Katie! Nothing more and nothing less. Amn't I right, Stephen?

STEPHEN You're right, Sylvie.

SYLVIE Bloody sure I'm right. Full complement, Eddie — united front! That scut Reilly back in his box and Captain Tansey back at the helm where he belongs.

EDDIE I'm delighted to hear it.

SYLVIE This calls for a drink! Hold the fort, Katie! (*Goes to parlour area*) In the immortal words of General Douglas MacArthur — I'll be back!

SYLVIE *exits.*

EDDIE How'd it go?

STEPHEN I did as you said. He only just made it.

EDDIE But he made it. I'd have given anything to see Reilly's face.

STEPHEN Let's just say he wasn't pleased. But it's a battle won, Eddie, not the war. And you know the price. Win or lose tomorrow night — he resigns next week.

EDDIE I know. We'll cross that bridge when we come to it.

SYLVIE *returns. Bottle and four glasses.*

SYLVIE Nineteen and sixty-three, Stephen!

STEPHEN Eighty-two, Sylvie.

SYLVIE Ye half eejit, ye. The *year*, I mean. Nineteen and

sixty-three.

STEPHEN What about it?

SYLVIE That was the year we bet the Strand Road boys off
the feckin' bandstand. D'y' remember?

STEPHEN Begod and I do, Sylvie.

SYLVIE (*Pours whiskey, distributes glasses*) The Sunday night
recital, Katie, their lot one week, ours the next, the
whole summer long. And — it need hardly be said
— fierce jealousy between the two outfits altogether.
We used to march from the bandroom, down
through the town and along the prom to the bandstand, so's you'd pull a crowd along the way. Only
one Sunday night didn't we notice we were pullin'
feck all and hardly a sinner to be found on the
streets? Amn't I right, Stephen?

STEPHEN That's right, Sylvie.

SYLVIE Well, bejaysus, it didn't dawn on me till we reached
the prom and heard the strains of *The Radetzky
March* wafting up to us from the far side. And there
they were, the scutter-arses from the Strand Road
perched on *our* bandstand for *our* recital!

STEPHEN The Parish Priest had died the week before, y'see,
and that week's recital cancelled as —

SYLVIE Am I telling this story or are you! They thought we
were going to give up our recital because they had
to give up theirs. Well, tough shite, says I, and dacent
of oul' Father Brennan to expire the week he did —
I always knew he was one of ours. The honour of
Garristown Brass is in the balance, men, says I. Are
we to turn on our heels and slinge home like a
defeated army or do we charge the bandstand and
fight the fuckers to the death? Well charge we did!
Struck up *The Minstrel Boy* to stir the blood, quick-
marched the length of the prom and laced into the
bastards like our lives depended on it. Begod, Katie,
'twas like a faction fight at a Fair Day. There was
tubas and bass drums and cornets flying in all direc-
tions but after the last blow was struck there wasn't
a man from the Strand Road left upright on that

bandstand.

EDDIE Tansey's finest hour!

SYLVIE (*Suddenly, without enthusiasm*) That's right — Tansey's finest hour. Nineteen sixty-three.

Silence.

STEPHEN (*Raises glass in a toast*) To victory!

ALL (*Except* SYLVIE) To victory!

SYLVIE (*Looks at them*) Yeah. To victory.

KATIE Jesus! You'll have to carry me home, Stephen.

STEPHEN No bother, Katie. And we'll drink again tomorrow, Sylvie. From the silver cup at Ballincollig.

SYLVIE Aye. The silver cup at Ballincollig.

STEPHEN Are ye right, Kate? Goodnight, Sylvie. Goodnight, Eddie.

EDDIE Good luck tomorrow, Stephen.

STEPHEN *nods. Exits.*

KATIE (*To* SYLVIE) I hope ye win tomorrow, Sylvie.

SYLVIE Please God — as they say. (*Goes to* KATIE. *Takes her hand*) We don't see enough of you, Katie. You'll call around for a chat sometime, won't you?

KATIE I will, Sylvie.

SYLVIE I'd like that.

KATIE (*Looking briefly to* EDDIE) Me too. We'll see ye, so. Goodnight, Da.

KATIE *exits.*

EDDIE I'm glad it went well for you.

SYLVIE Sentence deferred is all. Reilly had the look of a man was bidin' his time. Not the point though. I wasn't bested. And we played well tonight, that's the point.

EDDIE As long as you didn't peak too soon.

SYLVIE Don't you worry on that score, Eddie — that cup is as good as in the bag.

EDDIE I hope so. (*Pause*) It might be a good time to get out,

32

Sylvie.

SYLVIE What might?

EDDIE If you win, I mean.

SYLVIE Bollox.

EDDIE Why not? You said you wanted to go with your head high. The cup in one hand, your farewell speech in the other.

SYLVIE I'm not interested in their tuppenny-ha'penny cup. Not anymore, Eddie. We'll win tomorrow night but it'll be a means, not an end.

EDDIE A means to what?

SYLVIE To my resurrection, that's what.

EDDIE I don't understand.

SYLVIE No, you wouldn't. A part of me died the night you walked, Eddie. All-Ireland Champions, two years on the trot. If we'd won that year the cup was ours to keep. In *perpetuity*! D'y'know what that means, boy? That means forever. But you walked. And with such perfect timing, too. The night of the final rehearsal, the solo euphonium player's chair was empty.

EDDIE You know what happened.

SYLVIE I know we lost!

EDDIE You know why I wasn't there.

SYLVIE Yes! Yes, I know! That was the day you discovered Costello was shagging your wife.

EDDIE Such a way with words.

SYLVIE Well, they weren't playing bridge together, were they? She betrayed you and you betrayed me. Because when you walked you brought a little bit of me with you, Eddie. And I want it back. But it won't be found in Ballincollig. *Here*, y'see. In my own place is where I'll find it.

EDDIE You're talking in riddles, Sylvie.

SYLVIE It was never about winning — it was about striving for the best. (*Gestures to the music from the upstairs room*) *Listen*. A baker's son, you know. Luciano, I mean. Had the common touch and never lost it. But his voice, his voice, they say, touched by the hand of

God, touched by something greater than the baker's son could ever dream of. All the great ones are. And so they strive to sound the sacred note, the one that joins us with them and enables us to soar as well, to remember what is still possible on the other side of the mountain. (*Pause*) And I thought that in our own pathetic little way, this might be our function, too. That, however impoverished, our little band had a purpose in this place. And we did, too, Eddie — I wouldn't make too much of it but it was something. We were a conduit, a voice through which this town was enabled to sing and cry and celebrate and hope. We were a part of something, Eddie. And I want it back — just one more time I want to belong.

EDDIE The Regatta.

SYLVIE You said it, boy — means to an end. We win that competition and they wouldn't dare pass us over again.

EDDIE Does it mean that much to you?

SYLVIE Did it mean so little to you? *Community*, Eddie — and we were its ministers. You should have left this place and never come back because you betrayed them when you betrayed me. And they'll never forgive you for it.

EDDIE Will you?

Silence. SYLVIE *looks at him. Moves away.*

SYLVIE He sang in the church choir at Modena, you know. That's where he started. And his father with him by all accounts. That must have been nice. Father and son, side by side. They say he still goes back there. Each summer, returns to his native place and offers his gift again to his own. And I wouldn't wonder if he receives more than he bestows. Maybe no more than a memory, a drink again from the wellspring. But maybe, too, amongst his own, he remembers something else — the sacred purpose of his gift. That his voice belongs to those who have none, that when he sings, he sings for those who cannot speak. I like that. There's a form of symmetry in that exchange, don't you think?

EDDIE Good luck tomorrow, Sylvie.

SYLVIE Thanks. (*Pause*) Forgive *yourself*, Eddie. What I think won't matter much longer.

EDDIE I don't know what you mean.

SYLVIE You know what I mean.

SYLVIE *exits. Music plays on as lights fade.*

Scene Four

The same. Following night. Lights up on empty shop. After a moment, we hear voices offstage, singing. EDDIE *and* RITA *deliver a slow air and slightly strained version of 'The Holy Ground'. The door opens on the last line of the song.*

EDDIE Nobody home! That's a good sign, isn't it, Rita?

RITA I wouldn't read too much into it. You know that lot — win or lose, they'll have a drink in every village on the road from Ballincollig.

EDDIE No. They'd only be this late if they were celebrating.

RITA We'll see. (*Pause*) You still miss it, don't you, Eddie?

EDDIE What?

RITA The crack. The crates of beer at the back of the bus. Being one of the lads. They were good times, weren't they?

EDDIE I've had worse.

RITA Stephen said they worshipped the ground you stood on. He told me once you were the best musician the band ever had.

EDDIE Stephen is prone to exaggeration in that regard.

RITA Go on outa that. And no one loved you more than Sylvie, he said.

EDDIE Until I betrayed the tribe! Change the subject, Rita.

RITA Why do you keep hiding?

EDDIE I'm not hiding.

RITA Yes, you are. And you don't have to. Not from me.

EDDIE You must be tired, Rita. You should go home now.

RITA I'm not your enemy, Eddie. You don't have to do this on your own.

EDDIE Everybody's on their own.

RITA They don't have to be.

EDDIE Way of the world, Rita! Nature of the baste, as the oul' fella'd say.

RITA You loved him too, didn't you, Eddie?

EDDIE (*Silence*) Before the fall? I loved everybody before the fall. And *yes*, they were good times. And I *do* miss them! And he *did* think the sun shone out of my arse and I was fucking nuts about him, too! (*Quieter*) All of which is neither here nor there now. (*Pause*) We had a good night, Rita — don't spoil it.

RITA You weren't to blame, you know. Some day you're going to have to learn that. (*Goes to exit*) Mind yerself, Tansey.

EDDIE Rita. (*She stops*) Something I forgot to give you.

EDDIE *goes to her. Takes small box from his pocket, gives it to her.*

RITA What is it?

EDDIE Open it, for Jaysus' sake — it won't bite.

RITA (*Opens box*) Pearls are for tears, Tansey.

EDDIE Yeah, I know. Happy birthday, Rita — belated.

RITA You melt my bloody heart so you do! Just when I'm about to give up on you.

EDDIE You wouldn't do that, now, would you?

RITA Sometimes I think you want me to. (*Pause*) I never asked you for anything you didn't have to give, Eddie. But just now and again I stand at the edge of that line you drew and I look across at the other side and I wonder.

EDDIE I'm very fond of you, Rita.

RITA Yeah. Yeah, I know you are.

EDDIE That's something, isn't it? (*Silence*) We should dance.

RITA Why?

EDDIE I don't know why. Wouldn't do any harm, would it?

EDDIE *puts his arm on her shoulders. They begin to sway gently as, quietly, he begins to sing 'The Holy Ground' in slow tempo.* KATIE *enters from parlour. Unseen by* EDDIE *or* RITA, *she watches them dance. The song ends.*

KATIE Fine girl, y'are.

RITA Merciful Christ! You frightened the life out of me.

KATIE Will I go out and come in again?

EDDIE That won't be necessary.

KATIE Is there any news?

EDDIE Not yet.

KATIE That's a good sign, isn't it?

EDDIE Hope so. What are you doing back there?

KATIE I finished work at ten and came round to see if he was back. That parlour looks like a bomb dropped on it. I tidied it up while I was waiting.

EDDIE There was no need, Katie — That room went out of commission years ago.

KATIE There might be visitors. Some of the band might come back if they win.

EDDIE I wouldn't think so.

KATIE You'd never know. Did ye have a nice night, Rita?

RITA The best, Katie. Your father won't like me saying it but he's an oul' romantic behind it all. (*Goes to* KATIE *with pearls*) Look!

KATIE (*To* EDDIE) Pearls are for tears, Da.

EDDIE So I'm told. (*Shrugs*) Nobody's perfect!

SYLVIE *enters. Silence. Takes off jacket.*

So? How did it go?

SYLVIE Victory — was not ours, as they say. Our friends from the Strand Road took the honours. (*Pause. Gives jacket to* RITA) Must have been the uniforms. Never paid much heed to them, Rita, but they do confer a certain status, don't they?

RITA Would you like a cup of tea, Mr Tansey?

SYLVIE No. My poison is closer to hand. (*Whiskey*) Didn't touch a drop all day. Did it all by the book, Eddie, but to no avail. Still, we mustn't look back. (*Raises glass*) Here's to the future — and all who sail in her. (*Drinks. The others unsure what to say or do*) Will you cheer up, for Jaysus' sake — nobody died, did they?

EDDIE That's right, Sylvie, nobody died.

KATIE Master Reilly must have been pleased.

SYLVIE *Captain* Reilly now, Katie — I daresay he was. It doesn't matter. (*To* EDDIE) At least we know where we stand. There's always some virtue in clarity, isn't there?

EDDIE It's a lousy way to go.

SYLVIE It doesn't matter! We lost, it's over — there's no more to be said.

EDDIE You don't have to pretend with us, Sylvie.

SYLVIE There's no pretence. It's over, boy.

RITA C'mon, Katie.

SYLVIE No. Don't go, Rita. This is as close as we're ever likely to get to a family gathering. I know why you came back here, Eddie, and it's time we faced up to it.

EDDIE If I've explained that once —

SYLVIE Don't lie to me, please. It's my life — what's left of it. I wanted to go out singing, Rita — the spirit if not the body healed. But I was a fool. There *is* no resurrection, Eddie — before or after death. So, no more kid gloves, eh?

EDDIE (*Pause*) All right. No more lies, Sylvie.

SYLVIE I'll drink to that. You know the story, don't you, Katie?

KATIE Yeah. I know the story.

SYLVIE Good. That way we can cut through the bullshit. (*To* EDDIE) I take it my learned physicians were in touch?

EDDIE Yes.

SYLVIE So, what's the prognosis?

EDDIE Three or four months. Six, at the outside.

SYLVIE (*Clearly shocked*) I see. Well, at least it's summer. Let's hope it's a good one.

EDDIE They're not always right, Sylvie. You can't just lie down and wait.

SYLVIE What do you propose? An epic battle with the Angel of Death? This morning I had a reason to get up. Tomorrow I might find another one, but right now I can't think what it might be. I won't lie down but I won't fight either. I'll just wait, Eddie.

EDDIE And drink yourself to death?

SYLVIE A wonderful anaesthetic — you're not unfamiliar

with it yourself.

EDDIE   I won't watch you do that.

SYLVIE   Then don't.

EDDIE   That's no choice. You know I won't walk out on you.

SYLVIE   It wouldn't be the first time.

EDDIE   I want to give you something. (*Looks at* RITA) The thing I stole, maybe.

SYLVIE   You're too late. Twelve years too late.

EDDIE   If I owe you, I'll pay.

SYLVIE   With fucking what, boy?

EDDIE   I don't know yet.

SYLVIE   That's right. You don't know. So leave it alone, will you. Something happened back then. There was consequences. And something else is happening now. Just the way it is, that's all. And too late to change either of them.

EDDIE   We're in the salvage business.

SYLVIE   Then save your fucking self!

EDDIE   (*Silence. Quietly*) No. Us. Save us, Sylvie. Stephen says nothing is beyond redemption. It's a lovely word, isn't it?

SYLVIE   That's all it is. That band was my life.

EDDIE   Yes. I know.

SYLVIE   Do you? Do you, Eddie?

STEPHEN *enters, carrying instrument.*

STEPHEN   I saw the lights from the prom beyond. Just wanted to see you got home safe, Sylvie.

SYLVIE   My guardian angel! You didn't stay long at the wake then.

STEPHEN   I had no mind for it.

SYLVIE   Captain Reilly consumed by grief, no doubt?

STEPHEN   He's bearing up.

SYLVIE   And the rest of the troops?

STEPHEN   Porter is a great antidote.

SYLVIE   Indeed. But not for Stephen.

STEPHEN   No. Not tonight.

SYLVIE   Our faith, it seems, was misplaced.

STEPHEN We did our best.

SYLVIE Yes. There is that. But we didn't make it. Eddie and I were just talking about redemption. He tells me you're quite an authority on the subject.

EDDIE I didn't say that.

SYLVIE Don't be so pedantic. Stephen knows what I mean. So what price redemption now, Stephen?

STEPHEN We weren't disgraced, Sylvie. We gave a good account of ourselves.

SYLVIE We lost.

STEPHEN By two points. That's all was in it, Eddie.

SYLVIE Might as well have been twenty. We lost, Stephen, and Reilly's sweaty palm is on the baton. There's no redemption from that, is there?

STEPHEN (*As close as he'll ever get to anger*) I was proud of you, Sylvie. That mightn't mean much to you but I was. You didn't tell them everything, did you? How the hall stood and cheered when you went up for the prize?

SYLVIE Second prize!

STEPHEN (*Insistent*) How they stood and cheered, Sylvie! (*Quieter*) For two full minutes, Eddie — the bands of nine counties. Did you ever see the like of that in your time?

SYLVIE Empty fucking sentiment!

STEPHEN And what the adjudicator said? Did he tell ye that? How he was proud — no, privileged — to stand on the one stage as Sylvie Tansey — the finest bandsman of his generation.

SYLVIE Patronising bastard.

STEPHEN They were *his* words, Sylvie — not mine. He talked about the year of the fire in the bandroom, Eddie. How any other band would have gone under, how this one nearly did, only Sylvie pulled the master stroke that saved the day.

EDDIE The McCormack concert.

STEPHEN Even your own grandfather doubted him, Eddie — said the Count wouldn't sneeze, let alone sing, in a hole the like of this place. But you knew different, didn't ye, Sylvie?

SYLVIE Needs must, that's all. Nothin' to fuckin' blow about.

RITA It must have been a great night, Stephen.

STEPHEN Aye, it was. The Count was past his best, of course — died the same year, if I remember right — but just now and again he'd hit a note would make your skin crawl and you'd know why it was Sylvie had to have him. We packed the Town Hall that night, Katie, and bought the first of the new instruments on the strength of it. It was a slow crawl after — wasn't it, Sylvie? — but we made it.

SYLVIE That was a bloody lifetime ago, Stephen.

STEPHEN No, Sylvie — it was the blink of an eyelid. I remembered something else about that night. The band were to do the warm-up for McCormack, Eddie, and Sylvie's father asked me to play the solo cornet piece from Strauss' *Casanova*? D'y'remember it, Sylvie?

SYLVIE Music to die for — if you'll pardon the expression.

STEPHEN I wasn't too long in the band at the time and damn near lost me life at the prospect. I told the Captain I couldn't do it — didn't I, Sylvie? — but he wouldn't take no for an answer.

SYLVIE (*Being drawn in, despite himself*) 'It's not a request, Mr Kearney, it's an instruction!'

STEPHEN The very words. The night of the concert I stood on the stage and God forgive me but I hated every bone in his body for what he was putting me through. But just before the off, Sylvie pulled me to one side and he whispered something in my ear. Do you remember what you said, Sylvie?

SYLVIE An act of contrition?

STEPHEN Be *still*, you said. This isn't about you. This is about the music.

Silence.

SYLVIE Yes. It does all come down to that, doesn't it? You never put a foot wrong.

STEPHEN Because I listened to what you said.

SYLVIE You have the poet's heart, Kearney. You could be trusted.

>SYLVIE *begins to leave.*

EDDIE Will you play it for us, Stephen?

STEPHEN (SYLVIE *stops*) Now?

KATIE Good a time as any. I'd like to hear it.

STEPHEN (*Looking at* SYLVIE) I don't have the sheet music — we haven't played that piece in years.

EDDIE You don't need music — you'll remember. He'll remember, won't he, Sylvie?

SYLVIE (*Pause to* EDDIE) I daresay he will.

>SYLVIE *slowly climbs the stairs, enters his room. Silence.*

RITA It's late, Katie — I'll be down the prom with ye.

>KATIE *exits to parlour area for jacket.*

EDDIE (*To himself*) That when he sings, he sings for those who cannot speak.

RITA What?

EDDIE Thick as thieves, you know, the pair of them.

RITA Who?

EDDIE So the father says, anyway. Must have read about them somewhere, I suppose.

RITA Eddie, what in God's name are you on about?

EDDIE Luciano! Luciano and his old man. Sylvie says they sang together in the church choir at Modena.

RITA Who the bloody hell is Luciano?

EDDIE Luciano Pavarotti! Modena's where he comes from, see. Sylvie says he goes back there every summer and sings again for his own. I wonder is the oul' fella still in the choir?

KATIE Why don't you ring Luciano and find out?

EDDIE Because I haven't got his number.

RITA Yeah. Well, when you get it, give him our fond regards. Goodnight, Stephen. C'mon Katie.

EDDIE Question is, where would ye start?

KATIE Start what?

EDDIE Once the wheels are in motion, it'd take its own course, but where the hell would ye start?

KATIE Start what, Da? We might know the answer if we knew what the question was.

EDDIE Not to mention where we'd put him. Town Hall's out of the question, of course. Too small for starters, and the stink of them toilets. It would have to be outdoors. But where?

KATIE What!

EDDIE A concert! For Sylvie. Tansey Productions presents. For one night only, venue to be confirmed, Luciano Pavarotti in concert! (*Silence*) What d'yous think?

KATIE I think you're leaving us, Da.

EDDIE Maybe. But it'd be some crack, wouldn't it?

RITA Sure. And so will the Second Coming.

EDDIE Think of the surprise if it happened, though. We'll have to make a plan, Rita.

RITA Who's we?

EDDIE You said you wanted to help, didn't you? (*Goes to desk*) Pen and paper! Write it all down in black and white.

KATIE You're not serious, Da.

EDDIE (*Accent*) Wait and see, sweetheart. Now, first things first. First, we call a public meeting, announce our little venture to the good citizens of Garris.

RITA You *are* serious. You'll be the laughing stock of the town, Eddie.

EDDIE What's new? They said McCormack wouldn't come either but Sylvester above never blinked. Amn't I right, Stephen?

STEPHEN Not an eyelid, Eddie.

EDDIE Stubborn as a mule, them Tanseys, and this one, as you know better than most, Rita, is no exception.

RITA You haven't a prayer, Eddie.

EDDIE On the contrary, Rita — a prayer is all I have.

There'll have to be a committee, I suppose, some sort of a nod in the direction of democracy. Never mind, beggars can't be choosers. Sylvie in the chair though and yours truly as impressario taking fucking orders from no one — we'll get that straight from the start. (*Pause. Looks up*) You'll be secretary, Katie, and you my personal assistant, Rita — P.A. as I believe it's known in the trade.

RITA   I don't think so, Eddie.

EDDIE   (*Stops writing*) Thought you said you wanted to help.

RITA   You know what I meant.

EDDIE   No — what? (*Pause. No reply*) *This* is what *I* mean. Sylvie's song, Rita. He might be dying but he's not dead yet.

RITA   And you think Pavarotti's going to drop everything to sing in a field in Garris!

EDDIE   When he knows why, he just might, yes. I'll tell him why.

RITA   Even if you could pull it off, Pavarotti won't save him, Eddie.

EDDIE   I know that. But it would give the old fucker a reason to put his hat on. That would be something, wouldn't it, Rita?

RITA   For him or you?

EDDIE   (*Pause. Then ignores this*) The band'll perform too, Stephen. Support act, granted, but the biggest house they'll ever play to.

RITA   That would wipe a slate or two, wouldn't it?

EDDIE   Don't know what you mean.

RITA   Don't you?

EDDIE   No. Case closed. Certain conditions to the contract though. Uniforms optional for starters. Mr Sylvester Tansey on the baton for the main course and Master Reilly in the back row cornets for just desserts.

STEPHEN   The right place for him, Eddie.

KATIE   Do you really think you can do this?

EDDIE   (*Silence*) Yes I do. Because I have to, y'see. (*Pause*) I wasn't the first Tansey to leave an empty chair in the bandroom, y'know. He walked once too, didn't he, Stephen?

STEPHEN He was seventeen years old, Katie. The band saw him off at the station, his father conducting, the passage for New York in Sylvie's pocket.

EDDIE And over there, at the far side of the world, between the building sites and the boarding house, ten dollars in his pocket and time to kill, he walked one day up the steps of the great Metropolitan Opera House and encountered, as they say, his destiny. Ezio Pinza and Rosa Ponselle in Giordano's *Fedora* — he still has the programme above in the room. Words he didn't understand, a plot he couldn't follow — it must have been like walking off the edge of the world. But half a lifetime later, he told me how music spoke to him for the first time that night. How the music made sense of music itself, expressing everything he felt but never had words to say. It must have been a blinding revelation, Rita, but as aria after aria washed over him he remembered the little band in Garris. And, though it was a continent away, he saw that the difference was only of scale and form, that the Garristown Bandstand and the great temple of the Metropolitan Opera House were joyously and intimately linked in the same sacred purpose. He went to every opera, in every season, for years after. Spent every spare dime he had on records and spoke of the great singers like other men on the building sites spoke of baseball players. (*Pause*) And then he came home. He was haunted, y'see. Haunted by the image of his father conducting the band at the station, the old man's disappointment wrapped like a great black cloak around him. Fifteen years later, the Captain went to the great bandstand in the sky and Sylvie was there to take the baton. The prodigal son had nothing on him, Rita, but I know why he came back. I know what he was trying to do and I know what it cost him when I walked. So I do owe him. And time is not on our side. (*Pause*) I need your help.

RITA I don't know that I can, Eddie.

EDDIE Well let me know, won't you?

> EDDIE *sits at desk. Silence.* KATIE *takes up instrument case. Hands it to* STEPHEN.

KATIE Play the music, Stephen.

STEPHEN Will Sylvie mind?

KATIE He won't mind. He has the poet's heart, too.

> *Goes to* EDDIE *as* STEPHEN *takes cornet from case.*

International Enquiries.

EDDIE What?

KATIE You heard me. Pavarotti's number. That's where you start.

> STEPHEN *begins to play. Upstairs, lying on the bed,* SYLVIE *hears the music, resisting at first, but gradually embracing it, the memory at once fond and deeply painful. He rises from the bed and, facing directly out to audience, begins to conduct the piece. Downstairs, the others listen intently as the music continues. At a point to be judged,* STEPHEN'S *solo playing is joined by SFX of full band accompaniment,* SYLVIE, *as it were, invoking them in his memory as the piece plays out to the end. Silence. Then, instant blackout.*

ACT TWO

Scene One

The same Saturday afternoon, some weeks later. Upstairs, SYLVIE, *in bed. His condition has deteriorated and he is clearly weaker. He is listening to the band music which drifts up from the pier — it is the Saturday of the Garristown Regatta.* KATIE *enters below, goes upstairs to Sylvie's room.* SYLVIE *turns slowly to greet her.*

SYLVIE   Katie! A timely intervention — I was indulging in the commission of the eighth deadly sin.

KATIE   I thought there were only seven.

SYLVIE   No. Sentiment — that's the eighth — leaves all the rest in the ha'penny place.

KATIE   I'll remember that. (*Takes barley sugars from bag*) Here. Dad says you're livin' on 'em these days.

SYLVIE   Yes. Pathetic, isn't it? The only vice I have left — suckin' barley sugar.

KATIE   Go on outa that. How are you anyway?

SYLVIE   How do I look?

KATIE   You look fine.

SYLVIE   Then you're an even bigger liar than your father.

KATIE   Well, I can hardly see you in this light. It's like a bloody tomb in here.

SYLVIE   (*Pause. He looks at her*) I'm getting acclimatised. What time is it?

KATIE   Two o'clock. Did ye not get up today?

SYLVIE   Not yet. Maybe later. (*Pause*) You should be down at the Regatta — the races'll be starting soon.

KATIE   I'm not pushed. (*Pause*) That music must break your heart.

SYLVIE   The march of time, Katie — no room for sentiment, remember.

KATIE   The band passed the hotel on the way to the pier.

Reilly looked like the cat who'd got the cream.

SYLVIE And his new uniforms too, by all accounts.

KATIE They looked like they belonged to someone else.

SYLVIE No doubt they'll fit in time. Is your father below?

KATIE Nope. Not unless he's hiding.

SYLVIE I shouldn't be surprised.

KATIE Did he tell you I was working for Costello?

SYLVIE No, but Rita did. A sore thing when it festers.

KATIE You can say that again.

SYLVIE Like the bus to Kilmore — it will pass eventually.

KATIE There's days I'd love to put a spell on this town. That, when you'd all wake up from it, you'd remember nothing.

SYLVIE Is that the way?

KATIE It is. Then we could all start again from the beginning.

SYLVIE If only it were that easy.

KATIE You have to want it. You have to want it real bad.

SYLVIE A bit late for me, I'm afraid.

KATIE Is it?

SYLVIE (*Pause. He knows what she means*) At least you came out of it well.

KATIE D'you think so?

SYLVIE Bloody sure of it. A walking advertisement for broken homes.

KATIE I wouldn't say that.

SYLVIE I'm saying it. I know it wasn't easy for you, Katie. But you came through. And I'll give him this much, he was a good father to ye.

KATIE Most of the time! (*Pause*) You were too, Sylvie. To him, I mean.

SYLVIE No. Too hard, Katie. In here, I mean. The heart's a stone.

KATIE That's not true. You're an oul' softie behind it all, so y'are.

SYLVIE No. It's the truth. He'll tell you that if you ask him. She would too if she was here to say it.

KATIE Who?

SYLVIE Maggie Healy — your grandmother. Her anniver-

49

sary today, you know. I was thinking of her just now. They used to have the dances one time. She loved to dance, so she did, but we never went. Hard men didn't dance, y'see. Only one night, in my cups, I was persuaded. Just the once, she said. So we did. And because I was drunk, we danced all night. And she looked so beautiful and she was so happy. And I wanted to tell her something, Katie. (*Pause*) But I didn't. Nature of the baste, see. I didn't tell her anything.

KATIE   Maybe she knew. (*Pause*) Maybe my Dad does too, Sylvie.

SYLVIE   (*Without conviction*) D'you think so?

KATIE   He told me about the song you'd play for her. I'm sure she understood. (*Takes sweets from bedside. Gives him one*) Are you scared, Sylvie?

SYLVIE   Of what?

KATIE   Dying.

SYLVIE   Yes.

KATIE   Then you're not such a hard man, after all.

SYLVIE   Touché.

KATIE   (*Kisses him. Takes his hand*) I'll see you later.

SYLVIE   (*As she goes*) Katie.

She turns. Silence. Something he wants to say but doesn't. Hold this a moment. Music stops. Applause from pier.

Reilly's finest hour. You should go down. The races'll be starting.

KATIE   Yeah. I can hardly wait.

As KATIE opens door of Sylvie's room, EDDIE enters below, carrying a large cardboard box which he places near desk in office area.

EDDIE   (*As he enters*) Ask and it shall be given — seek and you shall find!

EDDIE *searches among the junk and extracts an ancient typewriter which he places on desk.*

Out you come, my beauty — your day is not yet done!

KATIE *reaches foot of stairs.* EDDIE *takes new typewriter ribbon from pocket, takes off old ribbon and replaces it during the following sequence.*

Ah, Katie, didn't know you were here. Is Sylvie okay?

KATIE He's all right — given the day is in it.

EDDIE Indeed. Rita should be here soon. It seems her cuisine is more acceptable to his palate than mine.

KATIE Nothing wrong with that, is there?

EDDIE (*Not rising to this*) Did I say there was?

KATIE I'm sorry I didn't make it to the meeting last night.

EDDIE I'm sure you had your reasons.

KATIE I was working.

EDDIE Of course.

KATIE Was there a big turn out?

EDDIE Small, but select.

KATIE How many?

EDDIE Difficult to say, really.

KATIE How many, Da?

EDDIE Four — approximately. Five, if you include Francey Flynn from the nut house at Oldcastle, but shur poor Francey was with us in body only — he spent most of the evening talking to the Pope. Then there was that geezer embezzled the Credit Union in Kilmore a few years ago. Said he'd passed his accountancy exams in the nick and would be honoured to act as Treasurer.

KATIE Who else?

EDDIE The Widow Forsey, resplendent in her weeds — her husband died in 1978. She was blissfully pissed and slept through the entire proceedings. And last, but by no means least, Reverend and Mrs Crawford from our separated brethren. Positively dripping with enthusiasm, the pair of them, and would be thrilled to row in if only — to quote Mrs Crawford — 'God hadn't called us to toil in another vineyard'. Apparently the Reverend is being transferred to Newtownards the week after next.

KATIE You must be disappointed.

EDDIE Not at all — Newtownards is welcome to 'em.

KATIE With the meeting!

EDDIE On the contrary, Katie — our gesture to local democracy has been painlessly observed! It's a one man show from here on in!

KATIE I don't suppose Pavarotti has been in touch, either.

EDDIE Not yet. Ex-directory, I'm afraid.

KATIE I thought you wrote to him.

EDDIE I did. Three weeks to the day — care of Modena, Italy. He's probably on tour.

KATIE It's not looking too good, is it, Da?

EDDIE All is not lost, Katie. One door never closes but another is flung open! I met Ramie Leahy this morning.

KATIE Who's he when he's at home?

EDDIE He's seldom *at* home! Holds court from dawn to dusk in Brennan's Bar beyond in Seafield. Cost me four half ones and a large stout for the privilege of his company, but it was worth it. They called him the Dancehall King, Katie — he's long since liquidated his assets in Brennan's but, twenty years ago, Ramie's name was on the licence of every dancehall from here to Carne.

KATIE So?

EDDIE So I figured if his grey matter wasn't entirely pickled, he might be able to help. And hey presto! (*Takes beer mat from pocket on which is scrawled a name and address*) Three half ones later I got him on the blower to a few contacts of his in London — and he delivered. (*Gives* KATIE *the beer mat. Reads by rote*) Mr Tibor Rudas, Katie. Rudas Enterprises, 454 Del Monica Street, Los Angeles, California 20045.

KATIE What about him?

EDDIE What about him? Luciano doesn't take a piss, let alone sing, without this guy's say so, that's what about him! He's Pavarotti's promoter, see. (*Brandishes beer mat. American accent*) This is the guy we gotta deal with, Katie! (*Crosses to desk, gestures to box he'd brought in earlier*) and *this* is how we're gonna do it! (*Takes fax machine from box*) Behold! Our passage to the stars! Letters and telephones a thing of the past, Katie — the facsimile transceiver is your only man! (*Takes machine from plastic covering*) If we're going to make an impression on old Tibor over there in LA, then this is the boy will do it.

KATIE (*Impressed*) It must have set you back a few bob.

EDDIE Free gratis, Katie! I did a sort of sponsorship deal with Fred Kelly's Office Supplies.

KATIE That was decent of him.

EDDIE Indeed. Most obliging. Mind you, I did have to jog his memory.

KATIE About what?

EDDIE About a year ago. Discreet little hotel in the midlands. Let's just say that if the Captain of the Garris yacht club ever got wind Fred was shaggin' his wife he'd be blackballed for life!

KATIE That's blackmail, Da.

EDDIE Indeed it is, Katie — Our need is great. He threw this (*mobile phone*) in for good measure, not to mention the headed notepaper.

KATIE What will you do if they say no?

EDDIE I never think about that.

KATIE They probably will, you know.

EDDIE What's this? Another doubting Thomas?

KATIE I believe in you, Da — maybe no one else will.

EDDIE Luciano will.

KATIE (*Doubtfully*) Yeah. I hope so.

EDDIE *Hope* is right, Kate. Now, I must prepare my epistle — for a small consideration the exchange in Kilmore are going to connect us to the outside world this afternoon. With a bit of luck, Tibor and me will be doing business before nightfall.

KATIE Have you told Sylvie?

EDDIE (*He has been feverishly active throughout the foregoing but this stops him. Silence*) Not yet. I will. Soon as old Tibor gives the word. (*Resumes activity but with less conviction*) You think I'm crazy, too, don't you?

KATIE Stark raving lunatic would be closer to the mark. (*Pause*) But then maybe there's a pair of us in it. I'll be back in a few minutes.

EDDIE You going to the Regatta?

KATIE Nope. That typewriter went out with the dance halls, Da. Mr Rudas wouldn't be too impressed.

EDDIE Maybe I should go back to Fred.

KATIE No. Fred's already paid for *his* pleasure. I won't be long.

KATIE *goes.*

EDDIE (*'Rehearses' letter*) Dear Mr Rudas. Dear *Tibor*! It is with great pleasure and anticipation that I find myself writing to you and I hope — I *trust* — this letter finds you as it leaves me — in good health.

STEPHEN *enters. He is wearing the band's new uniform and carrying instrument.*

The Minstrel Boy from the war doth come — and in full regalia, too.

STEPHEN I only thought to see himself as I was passing.

EDDIE He's in the west wing, Stephen. Go on up — he'll be glad to see you.

STEPHEN In this (*uniform*)?

EDDIE Sylvie knows the story.

STEPHEN (*Goes to stairs*) About the meeting last night, Eddie —

EDDIE (*This is an act*) Least said soonest mended, Stephen — though I won't pretend I wasn't disappointed!

STEPHEN I would have gone. You know that. Only 'twas a First Friday — old habits die hard, Eddie.

EDDIE You'll go straight to heaven, Stephen. Go on up now.

EDDIE *continues typing as* STEPHEN *climbs stairs and enters Sylvie's room.*

SYLVIE Stephen — me oul' segocia!

STEPHEN Howya, Sylvie?

SYLVIE I've been better. But you're a sight for sore eyes.

STEPHEN (*Sheepishly*) What do you think?

SYLVIE I think — I think you look magnificent, that's what I think. We should have done it years ago. Turn around! (STEPHEN *turns*) D'y'know if you had an arse to go with that trousers, there wouldn't be a dry knickers in Garris tonight.

STEPHEN Sylvie!

SYLVIE I'm serious — girls *love* a uniform!

STEPHEN Go on outa that. We took a terrible ribbing marching down the prom. Catcalls and wolf whistles and the devil knows what.

SYLVIE Plebeians, Stephen — no class. You look wonderful, so you do.

STEPHEN Thanks, Sylvie.

SYLVIE Credit where it's due now — Master Reilly has made quite an impression. Pulling the Regatta from under the noses of the Strand Road lads is not to be sneezed at, you know.

STEPHEN They say 'twas paid for. They say Reilly dropped a few pound from his own pocket to get the recital.

SYLVIE All's fair in love and war.

STEPHEN It's not the same though, is it? You never stooped that low.

SYLVIE (*Mischievous smile*) Didn't I? (*Pause*) It's not how the pudding is cooked but what it tastes like that matters, Stephen.

STEPHEN The sooner Captain Tansey is back in command, the better — uniforms or no uniforms.

SYLVIE Captain Tansey is not going back, Stephen — you know that as well as I do.

STEPHEN I do not. I'm obliged to remind you, Sylvie Tansey, that the committee never did accept your resignation. Reilly's only keeping the seat hot till you're well again.

SYLVIE Indeed. And, uncharacteristically, I was touched by the gesture. But that's what it was. I'm dying, Stephen, and you know it as well as I do.

STEPHEN (*Pause*) Aye. I do.

SYLVIE So, no more to be said on the subject. (*Pause*) Is the magnum opus nearing completion?

STEPHEN The Stations? I'm on the last of them. This time next week I'll have him in the tomb.

SYLVIE All over then, bar the shoutin'. Isn't it odd they finished on the down beat? A wonder now they never gave us the Resurrection.

STEPHEN They had their reasons, I suppose.

SYLVIE Oh, yes, I'm sure they had. (*Pause*) I used to go back from time to time, you know. To Church, I mean. You'd be passing of an evening and the lights or the music or whatever would pull you in. I'd stand at the back of the church and when they'd raise their voices, united in supplication, I'd raise mine with them — impostor though I was. The solace of community, I suppose. And lately, I've begun to imagine, Stephen, that the real tragedy was not so much that Big Daddy didn't exist but that he'd abandoned us as a bad joke — walked off the podium and abandoned us to our fate. What do you reckon?

STEPHEN Shur how would I know? I leave the big questions to them as wants to ask them.

SYLVIE Wise man.

STEPHEN Sometimes I think I hide behind it but I do like to keep it simple. Making the oul' pictures with the glass, blowin' a few notes on this yoke — there's worse things you could be doing, isn't there, Sylvie?

SYLVIE You're the wisest man I ever knew, Stephen Kearney. (*Takes his hand*) We walked the one road, didn't we?

STEPHEN Aye. We did. The band was back where it belonged today, but I could take no pleasure in it. It near broke me heart to see that bastard in your place.

SYLVIE That doesn't matter now.

STEPHEN But it does, y'see. There's a new order in, Sylvie, and these yokes (*uniform*) are only the thin end of the wedge. He's talking about majorettes next year — young wans in short skirts and high boots and pom-poms.

SYLVIE Might be just the tonic for you.

STEPHEN Do y'think so? The next thing he'll have us doin' little side steps like the Garda Band above in Dublin. More like performing monkeys than musicians.

SYLVIE Maybe that's what the people want, Stephen.

STEPHEN Maybe. But it's not what I want.

RITA *enters below, carrying a covered tray.*

RITA Hi. Is he above?

EDDIE Where else?

As RITA *crosses floor and climbs stairs:*

STEPHEN I'm thinking to jack it in myself, Sylvie.

SYLVIE *Festina lente*, Stephen — I'd hasten slowly if I were you. You may find you need it more than it needs you. Behind the shiny buttons and the fancy foot-work it will still come down to the music in the end. (RITA *enters*) Ah, Florence! Have you met Nurse Nightingale, Stephen?

RITA That's enough of your lip. Lunch-time, Sylvester!

SYLVIE I've been looking forward to it all morning!

RITA (*As she lays tray out on bed*) Less of the sarcasm too! The uniforms are lovely, Stephen.

SYLVIE See! I told you.

RITA You wouldn't recognise the half of them. Even Reilly looked vaguely human.

SYLVIE That's quite a transformation.

RITA Vaguely, I said! (*Napkin*) Chin up!

SYLVIE Yes, Nurse! I think I've met my match, Stephen.

STEPHEN Aye. And enjoyin' every minute. I'll leave you to it.

SYLVIE What's yer hurry? Nurse Nightingale never stays long.

RITA Not a minute longer than she needs to.

STEPHEN (*Embarrassed*) There's a function above in the band-room, for the day is in it.

SYLVIE You don't have to, Stephen. Restoring the Regatta to its rightful owners deserves to be celebrated.

STEPHEN Would you think of coming up for a while?

SYLVIE No. Another time, maybe.

STEPHEN Right, so.

STEPHEN *leaves, goes downstairs and out.* SYLVIE *isn't eating.*

RITA You not hungry?

SYLVIE No.

RITA A little is better than nothing.

SYLVIE I'm grateful for your kindness, Rita.

RITA The pleasure is all mine.

SYLVIE You'll look after them, won't you? When all this is over, I mean.

RITA It's not over.

SYLVIE No. But I can see the finishing post.

RITA I'll look after them.

SYLVIE (*He struggles with this*) You're a good woman, Rita. You mean more to him than he's able to show. You know that, don't you?

RITA Yes, I do.

EDDIE Only stunted, y'see. It's in the blood. I'd like to think that afterwards things might be different. That Eddie might learn to grow again. That he might find his peace, y'know.

RITA I hope you find yours, too, Sylvie. (*Pause*) Rest now. I'll see you later.

RITA *leaves the room and goes downstairs.*

EDDIE (*As she descends*) Yours sincerely, Eddie Tansey, Esquire, Chief Executive, Tansey Productions Incorporated! (*To* RITA, *who empties contents of dinner plates into bin*) You didn't stay long.

RITA He's tired. I'll call back later.

EDDIE   I didn't see you at the meeting last night.

RITA   No.

EDDIE   (*As he runs an extension lead from carpentry desk to fax machine*) I thought maybe I'd missed you in the crowd.

RITA   All five?

EDDIE   Whenever two or three are gathered! (*Pause*) I tracked down his promoter today, Rita. And look — a fax machine. It's progress, isn't it?

RITA   There'd need to be, Eddie — Sylvie's fading fast.

EDDIE   Do you think I don't know that?

RITA   This is all the time you have left with him — I'd be careful how I'd use it if I were you.

> KATIE *enters, brandishing aloft a case containing a laptop computer.*

KATIE   Voilà! The Apple of my eye!

EDDIE   What's that?

KATIE   The twentieth century, Da! One Apple Mac laptop computer. If we're going to impress Mr Whatshisname, we might as well give ourselves a fighting chance.

EDDIE   Who did *you* blackmail?

KATIE   You, you idiot! You bought it for me. Now move over! (*Enters password etc.*) How's Rita?

RITA   Okay. You said you'd be down — the fairground's packed on account of the Regatta.

KATIE   I'm sorry, Rita — we're up to our eyes here. Was he telling you? We got a contact for Pavarotti.

RITA   So I hear. (*To* EDDIE) I'd better go. Remember what I said, Eddie.

> RITA *leaves.*

KATIE   What's the matter, Da?

EDDIE   (*Who has been reflecting on exchange with* RITA) Nothing, Katie. (*Pause*) You don't have to do this, you know.

KATIE   I know. Maybe I want to. (*Picks up the letter from typewriter*) Is this the draft letter?

EDDIE   It's the *master* copy!

KATIE   (*Laughing*) C'mon so! You read and I'll type.

> EDDIE *takes the letter. The moment of doubt past, he reads with renewed conviction as* KATIE *taps his letter onto the laptop.*

EDDIE   Dear Tibor, *comma*. It is with great pleasure and anticipation that I find myself writing to you; *semi-colon*. I trust this letter finds you as it leaves me — *dash* — in good health. *Full stop*!

> *The lights snap out and the scene ends as* KATIE *types the full stop. We come down to a single lamp focussed on* SYLVIE's *bed, whilst the downstage area is lit only by the glow from the computer screen.*

Scene Two

Ten days later. The same. Morning. KATIE *continues typing through the scene break.* STEPHEN *enters and resumes work on the last of the stained glass panels. In the half-light of the break, the telephone rings on the fax machine and, as the lights come up, we hear the sound of a fax beginning to come through.* KATIE *and* STEPHEN *stop working and stare in wonder at the machine.* KATIE *goes to fax, pulls it off and reads it as we hear the voice, off, deliver its contents. Above them, in the bedroom,* SYLVIE *gets up from bed and gets dressed during the sequence to follow, his movements slow and strained.*

VOICE OFF Dear Mr Tansey. Further to your fax of the fifteenth, Mr Rudas has asked me to write to you conveying his regret that your proposal cannot be considered in the absence of detailed and verifiable pre-production budgets. Such budgets as would indicate clearly the capacity of an organisation of your scale to assemble, in advance, the very considerable financial and structural package involved in a project of this order. For reasons it is unnecessary to detail here, Mr Pavarotti, with the exception of limited engagements already in place, will not be touring in this current year. On behalf of Mr Pavarotti and himself, Mr Rudas sends his warm best wishes to yourself and to your father for his speedy return to good health. I remain, yours sincerely, Helène Goddard, Personal Secretary to Mr Rudas.

EDDIE *bursts into the shop, mobile phone to his ear.*

EDDIE That's right. Tansey. T-A-N-S-E-Y. Tansey Productions. I wrote to you last week concerning the forthcoming Pavarotti concert here in Garris. Yes. Garris with a G. The thing is I don't want to put you under pressure but a number of pasta manufacturers are already 'biting' on this one and I'd like your company to have first option. (*Pause*) Yes. Yes, money would help. Luciano doesn't come cheap, you know — that's more or less the point I was trying to make in my letter. (*Pause*) Confirmed? Well no, not quite. A few minor contractual details yet to be finalised — but then that's what we're paying those lawyers the fat retainers for, isn't it? (*Pause*) Well, of course, I'll revert with a copy of the contract — it should be here any day now. (*Pause*) Well, thank you. (*Venom*) And good luck to you, too! (*Switches phone off*) Well, at least he didn't say no.

KATIE Mr Rudas did.

She hands EDDIE *the fax. He reads it in silence.*

I'm sorry, Da.

EDDIE *Nil desperandum!* Opening salvos, Katie. Par for the course in this game.

KATIE They said *no*, Da.

EDDIE No, they didn't. Not *categorically*. Mr Rudas is testing the waters, that's all.

KATIE They want to see our money. We don't have any.

EDDIE Not yet. How're you getting on with those sponsorship letters?

KATIE This is number thirty-five.

EDDIE Any replies?

KATIE No.

EDDIE Well, here's another batch. Give me the old list. I'll call them.

KATIE You've *already* called them.

EDDIE *Well, I'll call them again!* (*Quieter*) We'll send them copies of the fax — at least it'll prove Pavarotti's people are talking to us.

KATIE And they'll go reaching for their cheque books on the strength of that?

EDDIE No. We don't need their money yet. Just the promise of it. Play one off against the other, see. Half a dozen serious pledges and Mr Tibor-fucking-Rudas will be singing a different aria, I can tell ye.

KATIE Da, did you not read the bloody letter? Even if we

could raise the money, Pavarotti's not touring this year.

EDDIE Not strictly true, Katie. (*Grabs fax*) 'Mr Pavarotti, *with the exception of limited engagements*', will not be touring this year. Limited engagements, see.

KATIE Yeah, Da. Already in place.

EDDIE Not the point, Katie! That means he's doing *something*, doesn't it? And *that* means there's still hope! Now run to Fred Kelly's and get forty copies of this yoke. (*Winks at her*) Tell him to put it on my account. We'll post them out as soon as you get back and I'll follow up on the blower in the morning. We persuade a few of *them* to sign up in principle, then I'll get back to Mr Rudas and persuade *him* to add one more 'limited engagement' to Luciano's schedule.

KATIE How, Da?

EDDIE (*Pause*) I don't know how. One thing at a time, Katie.

KATIE We don't *have* much time.

EDDIE Which is why you shouldn't be standing here talking to me! (*As* KATIE *goes*) Katie? Don't forget to tell Fred I was asking for him.

KATIE (*Sullen*) Yes — Boss!

KATIE *goes.*

STEPHEN I know you've a lot on your mind, Eddie, but Flannery's guest house were on again about them chairs. They were due a week ago.

EDDIE I know, I know. I'll get around to them.

STEPHEN It's too late — she cancelled the order this morning.

EDDIE Bitch. Any more good news?

STEPHEN The Rector was on from the church at Carne. You were to collect some furniture there last night.

EDDIE I'll do it tomorrow.

STEPHEN He wants it done today.

EDDIE Well, I can do it today! He'll have to wait.

STEPHEN If you don't mind me saying so, Eddie — you'd need to be careful. Get a name for that sort of carry on in this game and you're bunched.

EDDIE Thank you, Stephen. But the Salvage Shop isn't exactly my priority right now.

The door opens upstairs. SYLVIE *emerges from his room, dressed to go out. Everything stops for an instant below.* SYLVIE *begins to descend stairs, his footsteps slow and measured.* EDDIE *goes to him.*

Howya, Sylvie? (*No reply*) Here, let me give you a hand.

SYLVIE I can manage.

EDDIE All the same —

SYLVIE I can manage, I said.

STEPHEN Howya, Sylvie?

SYLVIE Never better. How goes the work?

STEPHEN Nearly there. Spit and a polish and the job is oxo.

SYLVIE Good. You'll let me know when they go up. I'd like to see them up.

STEPHEN You'll be the first, Sylvie.

SYLVIE Is Reilly behaving himself?

STEPHEN We're gettin' the measure of him.

SYLVIE No sign of the pom-poms yet then?

STEPHEN Not so far, anyway.

SYLVIE Eddie tells me the band has the Hurling Final next month.

STEPHEN That's the rumour.

SYLVIE Excellent! A progressive return to the bosom of the community.

STEPHEN You might get along on the day, Sylvie.

SYLVIE I wouldn't count on it. You'll give them all my regards, won't you?

STEPHEN Indeed and I will, Sylvie. As a matter of fact they were asking for you, too. You were on the agenda at the committee meeting last week.

SYLVIE Under funeral arrangements, no doubt.

STEPHEN Go on outa that. There's talk of a tribute night at the Town Hall. Gala concert sort of thing. (*Pause*) They asked me to sound you out.

SYLVIE Did they now?

STEPHEN They did. Nothin'll happen without your say so, mind, but the lads are anxious —

SYLVIE To say goodbye?

STEPHEN To say thanks, Sylvie. (*Pause*) You might think about it.

SYLVIE I will. (*To* EDDIE, *brusquely*) I can't find me cap.

EDDIE Are you going out?

SYLVIE No, I just like dressing up. What d'you think I'm doing?

EDDIE There's a chill in that wind. Looks grand from here but nippy enough outside. Amn't I right, Stephen?

STEPHEN It's true, Sylvie. You'd want to wrap up well.

SYLVIE (*Slowly. Annoyed*) That's why I'm lookin' for me cap.

EDDIE (*Goes to drawer in 'office'*) There's one here somewhere. (*Tentatively*) Where y'off to anyway?

SYLVIE Nowhere in particular.

EDDIE I'll bring the car round. We could go for a spin.

SYLVIE I don't *want* to go for a spin. I *want* to go for a walk. Is that so unusual?

EDDIE You haven't been out for over a month, Sylvie.

SYLVIE All the more reason, I would have thought. (*To* STEPHEN) Jesus, when I'm in bed he wants me out, when I get up he wants me back again. (*To* EDDIE) Is there no fucking pleasin' ye?

EDDIE I'm sorry.

SYLVIE You don't have to be sorry! I just want to breathe some air. That's not a crime, is it? (*Pause*) What's this contraption?

EDDIE It's a fax machine.

SYLVIE Begod! There's posh for ye, Stephen. Did we ever think we'd see the likes of that yoke in the Salvage Shop?

STEPHEN (*A glance at* EDDIE) We did not, Sylvie.

EDDIE It's not *for* here.

SYLVIE Then what's it for?

EDDIE It belongs to Tansey Productions. That's me, Sylvie. It's for the concert.

SYLVIE What concert?

EDDIE The Pavarotti concert. (*A glance to* STEPHEN) Did I

not tell you about it?

SYLVIE Well, it's hardly the sort of thing would slip your mind, is it?

EDDIE It was your McCormack stunt put me in mind of it. I'm bringing Pavarotti to Garris, Sylvie. You did the impossible once, we could do it again, eh?

SYLVIE *We*, Eddie?

EDDIE I thought you might like to help.

SYLVIE Certainly! Stephen and me will sell tickets for the half-time raffle, won't we, Stephen?

STEPHEN Oh now, Sylvie, you'd never know.

SYLVIE Indeed you wouldn't! And are we permitted to ask when the great tenor is due to appear?

EDDIE That's still under negotiation. Just a few minor details, that's all.

SYLVIE Yes. (*As he begins to leave*) Well, I'm sure you'll keep me posted.

EDDIE I could do with your help, Sylvie.

SYLVIE No disrespect, boy — but I have other things on my mind, right now.

STEPHEN (*Checks silently with* EDDIE *as* SYLVIE *exits*) Sylvie? (SYLVIE *turns*) I have an appointment above in the church. Would ye mind if I walked the road with ye?

SYLVIE (*A glance at* EDDIE. *He knows what they're up to*) No. No, I wouldn't.

> SYLVIE *exits.* STEPHEN *grabs jacket, a nod to* EDDIE *and quickly exits after* SYLVIE. EDDIE *alone, obviously upset by both his father's condition and the encounter with him. Then he buries this. Sings 'The Minstrel Boy' through gritted teeth as he crosses back to desk.*

EDDIE His father's sword indeed. Never mind! The show must go on. (*Types the following*) Dear Sirs, Further to my letter of last week —

> COSTELLO *has entered.* EDDIE *becomes aware of his presence. Stops typing. Clearly shocked.*

COSTELLO Hello, Eddie.

EDDIE We're closed.

COSTELLO The door was open.

EDDIE Not to you, it isn't.

COSTELLO Predictable as ever, Eddie.

EDDIE Get out — before I kick you out.

COSTELLO Ah, Eddie, there's no call for that. Those old wounds must be well licked by now. Besides, wounds are one thing and business is another.

EDDIE I have no business with the likes of you, Costello.

COSTELLO You'd never know. (*Looks around him, wanders about, examining furniture, bric-à-brac etc*) Was that the Daddy I saw headin' up the prom just now? A pity to miss him — I always admired old Sylvie, y'know. Tough as boots, of course, but fair behind it. That's what counts, isn't it, Eddie?

EDDIE What do you want?

COSTELLO I hear he's not well.

EDDIE What he is or isn't is no concern of yours.

COSTELLO True. Still, I'm sorry for your trouble, Eddie — it's not an easy thing to watch, is it?

EDDIE I don't want your fucking sympathy.

COSTELLO Sincerely offered nonetheless. A shame about the band, too. There's no denyin' it, Eddie, but it's a hard station. A man gives his life to something he loves and, when he's on his last legs, they kick him out the door.

EDDIE What do you want, Costello? If you've something to say, then say it and get the fuck off my property.

COSTELLO Steady, Eddie, steady! It's not what *I'm* lookin' for that brings me here. By Jesus, you mightn't be one for surprises but when you go for it you sure come up trumps. I can see the headlines already — Pavarotti Comes to Garris! Credit where it's due, Eddie, that's one helluva notion you have there.

EDDIE There must be something wrong with it if you're impressed.

COSTELLO Nothin' that can't be mended.

EDDIE *busies himself with some activity or other but is clearly troubled by* COSTELLO's *presence.*

Pity about the turnout at the meeting last week. The Widow Forsey won't be much addition to ye, not to mention poor Francey. You deserved better than that, Eddie. Reminds me of the time I bought the big house at Edenvale. Costello's Folly they christened it. There's eighty bedrooms up there now — the biggest leisure centre on this coast. That's called vision, isn't it, Eddie?

EDDIE You're an inspiration to us all.

COSTELLO Do you think so? I'm touched. The point is you could get the same result — if you box clever. The question is, can you box?

EDDIE Is that the way?

COSTELLO I'm only calling it like I see it, Eddie. What you have on your hands is an idea that could make Garris the talk of Europe. But that's all you have — no structure, see. And maybe that's where I come in.

EDDIE Close the door behind you.

COSTELLO Think about it, Eddie — your imagination and my brains — not to mention money and a site. We could make it happen, Eddie.

EDDIE It's *going* to happen. But when it does, it won't owe anything to the likes of you.

COSTELLO We don't have to do this for the same reason, you know. You have your motives, I have mine. Now, I've been making some enquiries about how these things operate and what it comes down to is this: a site, a series of sponsorship deals and the expertise to stage the gig to Mr Pavarotti's quite properly exacting requirements. A hundred grand up front should convince them we're serious and that's when the real talking starts. The next thing we need is a site.

EDDIE The grounds of Edenvale, no doubt.

COSTELLO Have you come up with anything better? There's a thirty-acre field between the house and the sea —

it's a natural amphitheatre.

EDDIE   Such a big word for such a little man.

COSTELLO   I can spell it, too.

EDDIE   You're a rat, Costello — go back to the hole you crawled from.

COSTELLO   Sticks and stones, Eddie — I've been called worse. I'll go all right but when I walk out that door you'll be looking at the only man you'll ever know could have made your little dream come true.

EDDIE   I forgot. That's your speciality, isn't it? That's what you told her, too. She was a third-rate cabaret singer in your seedy little hotel, but you were going to make her a star. Isn't that what you promised, Costello?

COSTELLO   Maybe I did, maybe I didn't.

EDDIE   Oh you did, all right. I remember because she told me. He believes in me, she said, and you don't, Eddie, that's why I'm leavin' ye. I never stood a chance, did I, Costello? Except for one thing — you didn't deliver. You destroyed her instead.

COSTELLO   If that's what you need to believe —

EDDIE   That's what happened, Costello.

COSTELLO   In *your* opinion.

EDDIE   *That's what happened!*

COSTELLO   Not quite, Eddie. If you want to tell a story you have to start at the beginning. And the beginning of that particular story is that if I hadn't shagged your wife, then someone else would have.

EDDIE, *enraged, grabs* COSTELLO *by collar and raises his fist to punch him. But doesn't.*

Go ahead, Eddie — Christ knows, you've been waiting long enough. Go ahead — if it makes you feel better. (EDDIE *releases him. Pushes him away*) No, I didn't think it would. Because I wasn't the problem. You were. And you know it — just like she did.

RITA *enters.*

RITA   (To EDDIE) I didn't know you had company.

EDDIE   That's not what I'd call it. Mr Costello is just leaving.

COSTELLO   Hello Rita. Long time no see.

RITA   (*To* EDDIE) I saw Sylvie on the prom with Stephen. I'll change the sheets while he's out.

RITA *goes to parlour.* COSTELLO's *eye follows her out.*

COSTELLO   A woman's touch. You can't beat it.

EDDIE   (*Calm, measured*) You're slime, Costello. I *know* you. Every move you've ever made and why.

COSTELLO   I'm flattered.

EDDIE   Yeah? It's no more than the minor obsession of a jilted husband. But I *do* know you. You have it all sussed, don't you? You just snap your grubby fingers and the world comes dropping at your feet. Habit of a lifetime, I suppose — but not this time, Josie, not *this*. Because this is different, see — this is *class*. So you can leave your cheque book in your pocket because, believe it or not, there's still one or two things your money can't buy.

COSTELLO   Tansey Productions! Jesus! A fucking fax machine and a battered typewriter operating out of a second-hand furniture store. Is that what you call class?

EDDIE   Yeah. Yeah, it is actually. But I wouldn't expect you to understand that.

COSTELLO   And Mr Pavarotti will, I suppose.

EDDIE   We'll see.

COSTELLO   You're a fucking nobody! Always were and always will be. That's why your missus did the runner, Tansey — nothing to do with me. She saw the writing on the wall and jumped. I just happened to be there to break her fall.

EDDIE   Is that what you call it — breaking her fall?

COSTELLO   Yes! And she was glad of it.

EDDIE   She sure is glad of it now.

COSTELLO   That's another story. Not that it's any of your business, but when my little fling came to light, Kathleen and me and Mrs Costello came to an understanding. In my society that's called discretion, Tansey. It wasn't my fault Kathleen couldn't stay the distance.

EDDIE The killer touch. You never lost it, did you, Costello?

COSTELLO No. And I'm sure I never will. Here's my card, Tansey. Business is still business. Oh, and remember this — your little enterprise doesn't have a patent on it. I know why you're doing it, so call it the goodness of my heart that I'm here — but I don't actually need you at all. Give me a call when you change your mind.

EDDIE You'll be waiting.

COSTELLO I can wait. Can you? (*Pause*) By the way, give my regards to Sylvie.

EDDIE (*As* COSTELLO *goes*) She still sings, Costello.

COSTELLO *stops.*

Yeah. Imagine that. Nothin' fancy, mind. Not the sort of stuff you promised her. Back room of a bar in Harlesden, first Saturday of every month. Not exactly the Albert Hall, is it, but she still sings! And because you don't know what that means, you'll never know what this means, either.

Pause. COSTELLO *goes. We hear 'La Donna e Mobile' from Verdi's* Rigoletto *as* RITA *emerges from the parlour to witness* EDDIE *pick up Costello's card and tear it up. They look at each other in silence as music continues and lights fade.*

Scene Three

The same. A week later. Afternoon. In the bedroom, SYLVIE asleep. Below, STEPHEN is preparing a packing case to receive the last of the stained glass panels. EDDIE is sitting at office desk, with feet up. Letters strewn across desk, which he idly crumples into paper balls and aims at a nearby wastepaper basket.

EDDIE   (*As he does*) No. (*Pause*) No. (*Pause*) And no! Guy walks into Fagin's Bar this morning, Stephen. Orders a pint of Guinness. Barman gives him the pint, the guy throws two pounds and two fivers onto the counter. The barman takes the two quid, asks the guy what's the story on the two fivers. That's not two fivers, the guy replies, that's a tenor for Eddie Tansey! (*Pause*) Not bad, eh?

STEPHEN   Must have brought the house down.

EDDIE   At least I've put a smile on the faces of the local peasantry.

STEPHEN   They laughed at Sylvie, too, the time of McCormack.

EDDIE   True. The difference is, Sylvie delivered.

STEPHEN   You might too, Eddie.

EDDIE   Not if corporate Ireland has anything to do with it. That's the last of the list in the bin.

        KATIE *enters in a fury.*

KATIE   *You might at least have bloody well told me!*

EDDIE   Told you what, my precious?

KATIE   *You know what!* I came round here this morning to open the post — same as I've done every day since you roped me into this. You weren't here, of course, you had far more important things to be doing. Like drowning your bloody sorrows in Fagin's Bar! In case you didn't bother reading them, there were three more regrets today.

EDDIE   I read them. The last of the list.

KATIE   That's right. Thirty-five of them. I ought to know

because I typed the bloody letters in the first place. You can imagine my disappointment, can't you, Da. Only unlike you, I didn't have time to drown my sorrows — I had to go to work. So I spend the morning racking my brains trying to figure out what the hell we're going to do next. I tell myself there's got to be an answer, Katie, you just have to look harder, that's all. And then the answer walked in the door. If I'd stopped to think I'd probably have done nothing. But I didn't stop. I just went right on up to him and asked if I could see him for a minute. Of course, says Mr Costello, I've been meaning to talk to you, too. *You can guess the rest!*

Silence.

EDDIE   Yes.

Stephen   I'll be off, so, Eddie.

KATIE   I'm sorry, Stephen. You shouldn't have to listen to this.

STEPHEN   I've heard worse. (*To* EDDIE) They'll send for the windows in due course. (*As he goes*) All ye have is each other, Katie. Remember that.

STEPHEN *exits.*

KATIE   Too bloody right, Stephen. I trusted you, Da. I believed in you when no one else did. I didn't care if it was Pavarotti or the Pope or the Lord Mayor of Shanghai was going to drop out of them skies — I would have opened the gates of hell to make it happen. And d'y'know why, Da? Because it might have set you free.

EDDIE   (*Goes to kitchen area*) Time for his Complan. We're down to that.

KATIE   That didn't seem to matter much when it came to swallowing your pride, did it?

EDDIE   (*Controlling himself*) Five different flavours, you know. We'll try strawberry today!

KATIE Listen to me! You think I enjoyed going cap in hand to that bastard. I *know* what he is. I *know* what he did. But I don't care, Da. I'm not trapped, see. You're the one who's really in his keep. I took his job because it suited me and if it's not too bloody late I'll take his Pavarotti money as well.

EDDIE And I won't.

KATIE No? Then it wasn't so important after all.

EDDIE You don't know what you're talking about, Katie.

KATIE Don't I? Well how's this: I think it was more than your pride that stopped you. I think you like your chains. You've been wearing them so long, they'd only hurt now if you took them off. Well, too bad, Buster, there's a price on what you say you want and you're going to have to pay it.

EDDIE Not to him.

KATIE Yes, to him! He's our last chance.

EDDIE No. There's still time, Katie. We just have to look harder, that's all.

KATIE Costello has what we're looking for, Da! All you have to do is reach out your hand and take it.

EDDIE I *can't*! (*Silence*) I loved her, see. You and me and her against the world. And he destroyed that. You want me to shake his hand and pretend it never happened?

KATIE No. I wanted you to let go. Maybe I don't understand. Maybe you need those chains more than I thought. But you better explain that to Sylvie when Luciano doesn't show up.

EDDIE Sylvie doesn't care one way or the other.

KATIE Not now, he doesn't. You said yourself he'd come round if we got the green light. Knowing Sylvie, he'd have ended up doing Master of Ceremonies. (*Pause*) You'd better bring him up his Complan.

    Silence.

EDDIE Sylvie conducts the band.

KATIE What?

EDDIE You heard me. The band does the warm-up. Sylvie conducting. Tell Costello I want that on paper if the concert goes ahead.

KATIE (*Pause*) I'll see what I can do.

EDDIE On *paper*. And his name on the poster. Tansey Productions Presents —

KATIE (*Pause*) I'll see what I can do.

EDDIE (*As* KATIE *goes*) There's a part of this his money can't buy, Katie.

KATIE You think I don't know that?

> KATIE *goes.* EDDIE *remembers Sylvie. Fetches Complan, tablets, water, puts the lot on a tray and goes upstairs.* SYLVIE *wakes, glances at* EDDIE, *then at tray and then away.*

EDDIE (*Struggling for the up beat*) Never fear, Nurse Tansey is here! Lunch-time, Sylvie! Better late than never, eh? (*Silence*) Yes. (*Hands him water*) There you go, red and green for starters — if we had a little yellow one we could play traffic lights.

SYLVIE Your bedside humour leaves a lot to be desired, Eddie.

EDDIE We can but try! (*Takes glass back*) Merci beaucoup! And now, chef's special: Complan au Lait — in your favourite strawberry flavour! (*Pause*) So, how's the patient?

SYLVIE He's all right.

EDDIE Any pain?

SYLVIE Nothing I can't manage. The morphine will probably get me before the cancer. (*Gestures to mug*) Though this stuff will give them both a run for their money.

EDDIE Don't knock it, Sylvie — it has all the nutrition of a three course meal! It says so on the packet.

SYLVIE Does the packet say it tastes like shite?

EDDIE Vanilla tomorrow, so!

SYLVIE I can hardly wait.

EDDIE I'm not much good at this, am I?

SYLVIE A little less of the forced gaiety, maybe.

EDDIE I shall introduce a note of gravitas, forthwith. (*Pause*) Are you getting up?

SYLVIE No.

EDDIE I thought we might go for a walk.

SYLVIE Not today.

EDDIE The length of the prom even — the air would do you good.

SYLVIE D'you think so?

EDDIE Maybe tomorrow. (*Gets up. Goes to window*) We'll let the light in, at least. You can see what you're missing.

SYLVIE I *know* what I'm missing.

EDDIE (*Window remains closed*) As I said, maybe tomorrow. (*Pause*) Stephen tells me you've given the go-ahead for the tribute night.

SYLVIE I didn't have much choice.

EDDIE Sylvie Tansey never did anything he didn't want to do. (*Pause*) Are you looking forward to it?

SYLVIE A necessary ritual, that's all. Allows Reilly and his foot-soldiers put their consciences to rest.

EDDIE It gives Garris a chance to say thanks as well.

SYLVIE For what?

EDDIE You know for what.

SYLVIE Here. That's about as much of this as I can stomach. I'll see you later.

EDDIE Sylvie?

SYLVIE I'm tired, Eddie.

EDDIE I know. This won't take a minute. There's been a breakthrough, Sylvie.

SYLVIE What? Have you come back to your senses?

EDDIE It's not just me anymore, I've found an investor.

SYLVIE They say there's a fool born every minute.

EDDIE Yeah? Well this one is prepared to put up a hundred grand.

SYLVIE Who is this fucking eejit?

EDDIE Josie Costello.

SYLVIE Jesus. You're even further gone than I thought.

EDDIE Beggars can't be choosers, Sylvie. The point is, he can make it happen. And something else — I've stitched the band in as the warm-up act for Pavarotti.

SYLVIE   I hope it keeps fine for ye.

EDDIE   Maestro Sylvester Tansey on the baton, if you please.

SYLVIE   Sure. And maybe I'll do a duet with the Big Fella as well.

EDDIE   It could be arranged. It's not makebelieve anymore, Sylvie.

SYLVIE   (*Explodes*) What do you want me to do — get up and dance a jig? This isn't makebelieve either, boy! I'm fucking dying! And you getting into bed with that bastard so you can spend a few more days in cloud-fucking-cuckoo-land isn't going to take the sting out of that.

EDDIE   Costello is just the means, that's all.

SYLVIE   To what?

EDDIE   You know what.

SYLVIE   No. Tell me, Eddie. Say it.

EDDIE   The concert. The Pavarotti concert. You know that.

SYLVIE   But why? Why are you doing this, Eddie?

EDDIE   It doesn't matter why.

SYLVIE   Yes it does. Now fucking tell me.

EDDIE   Passing the time, that's all. Bit o' crack on the summer evenings.

SYLVIE   More than that, Eddie!

EDDIE   No! No more than that.

SYLVIE   The truth, Eddie — *say it*!

EDDIE   *All right*! All right, Sylvie! It's for you. For me and you. For what I owe you. Something between this and the dark, that's all.

SYLVIE   I told you before, you don't owe me anything.

EDDIE   No. The euphonium player's chair was empty. But I'm back, Sylvie.

SYLVIE   With the world's greatest tenor tucked under your wing. It's too late for that.

EDDIE   No. You mustn't say that. Something to look forward to.

SYLVIE   *Look at me, boy*! A bag of bones in a dark room. Slow fade to blackout, that's what I'm looking forward to. Does Pavarotti have a song for that?

EDDIE We'll see, Sylvie.

SYLVIE I *do* see! I've never seen more clearly, Eddie. The way it *is* though. I told you I wouldn't fight this but I did. I tried to. You think I wouldn't have liked to walk that prom with you today? You know why those curtains are drawn? Because I can no longer bear to look. At all that *life*! At the colour of it. The energy of it. The fucking wonder of it! I'm jealous of what's out there because it doesn't belong to me anymore. So I do *see*, Eddie. Exactly what's in front of me. Where I am and where I'm going. And I don't like it one fucking bit. But a dozen bloody Pavarottis aren't going to save me from it. Go ahead. Do it! But not for me. Save yourself, Eddie. Just let me sleep.

Long silence. EDDIE *watches* SYLVIE *intently. Downstairs,* RITA *enters, carrying a bunch of flowers. She goes out to parlour and returns directly with vase in which she places and arranges flowers.*

EDDIE So be it. Sleep, Sylvie. Sleep in peace. (*Goes to stereo. Turns it on. 'E lucevan le stelle' from Puccini's* Tosca) And music, Maestro! The music will help you sleep. That's what it was *for*, y'see.

EDDIE *leaves room and descends stairs as we continue to hear Pavarotti from the room above.*

RITA Is he all right?

EDDIE (*Nods*) He's sleeping.

RITA I met Katie. She told me the story.

EDDIE There *is* no story. Not anymore. He just wants to sleep. I'll let him sleep. I suppose that's how it was always going to be. The days passing, the light falling, the slow grinding to a stop. I should have listened to you, Rita. I know it was stupid but I thought somehow Luciano was going to descend from the skies and save us.

RITA As Sylvie said, you have to believe in something, don't you? It's you he needs now, Eddie, not Pavarotti. And you need him, too. I'd forget the grand gesture though — small steps are more suited to your style. From what I hear, you already took one today. Who knows — you might be up to a few more.

EDDIE (*Goes to* RITA. *Rests his head on her shoulders*) I'm scared, Rita.

RITA And so you should be. (*Takes his hand*) But you're not on your own, Eddie. Sylvie isn't either. Not any-more.

> RITA *embraces* EDDIE. *The embrace becomes a slow dance. The lights fade and the music soars to end the scene.*

Scene Four

The same. A week or so later. Night. EDDIE *alone at the office desk, lit only by the faint glow from the computer screen.* KATIE *enters carrying hold-all.*

KATIE Hello.

EDDIE Hello Katie.

KATIE What're y'up to?

EDDIE Nothing. (*Turns on light over desk*)

KATIE Did you not go back to the bandroom?

EDDIE No. Couldn't quite rise to that.

KATIE Me neither. It was a good night, wasn't it?

EDDIE Yeah. Never saw the town hall so packed. Sylvie must have been thrilled.

KATIE Despite himself! (*Pause*) Are you glad you went?

EDDIE Wouldn't have missed it for the world.

KATIE I told Sylvie I saw you. He didn't say much but I know he was pleased — even if you did stand at the back of the hall! (*Pause*) I was talking to Costello, Da. Pavarotti won't be coming.

EDDIE Is that so? Hardly a surprise at this stage.

KATIE He's playing Dublin next year. They won't consider anything before then.

EDDIE Of course. Mr Costello must be disappointed.

KATIE On the contrary. He's meeting some of Rudas' people in London next week to talk about sponsorship. He thinks he can persuade Pavarotti to stay at Edenvale when he comes over.

EDDIE No doubt he will, too. It's an ill wind, Katie. I'll get this (*fax*) back to Fred in the morning — we won't have much use for it here.

KATIE (EDDIE *packs the machine into its box*) I'm sorry, Da.

EDDIE It doesn't matter. It wouldn't have changed anything, Katie.

KATIE I know what you were trying to do.

EDDIE Yeah. Just had the wrong tools, that's all. Thanks for your help.

KATIE   There were things I said last week —

EDDIE   Yesterday's news, Katie. And message received, loud and clear. I'll work on it — I promise you that. (*Puts fax-machine box on floor. Notices Katie's gear*) Where you off to?

KATIE   I quit the hotel tonight.

EDDIE   How come?

KATIE   Just felt like it.

EDDIE   Why, Katie?

KATIE   Because I want to come home.

Pause.

EDDIE   I see. As long as you know it's your decision.

KATIE   I know.

EDDIE   You still have a key for the flat?

KATIE   I'm staying here, Da.

EDDIE   No.

KATIE   Why not?

EDDIE   No room.

KATIE   There's a sofa bed in the parlour. You said no one ever goes in there.

EDDIE   *There's no room*, Katie! I don't want you staying here.

KATIE   Why not, Da? Afraid I'll end up like you?

EDDIE   Maybe. Like me and him. Drowning in our own poison. You hang around here, Katie — we'll poison you, too.

KATIE   I'll take my chances on that. (*Pause*) I was proud of him tonight, Da. And proud of you for having the courage to go there. I didn't feel poisoned.

EDDIE   You don't know everything, Katie! It was a good night. I'm glad he enjoyed it, I'm glad I was there — none of it was any more than he deserved. But tomorrow it's just me and him again. Lights off and into the dark. I don't know what's going to happen on the way.

They are interrupted by the voices offstage of SYLVIE, RITA *and* STEPHEN *singing 'La donna e mobile' from*

Verdi's Rigoletto. SYLVIE, *who is now in a wheelchair,
is rolled in by* STEPHEN, *followed by* RITA, *who wears
Stephen's uniform hat. They circle the stage,* SYLVIE
*wielding baton, and come to a halt on the last line of
the song.*

SYLVIE (*Looks at his watch*) Nine minutes — and fifty-two
seconds! We did it, Stephen — eight seconds to
spare!

STEPHEN (*Breathless*) I wouldn't doubt ye, Sylvie. You're a
man of your word.

KATIE What in the name of God are ye up to?

SYLVIE It's a new world record, Katie. Quick march from
the bandroom to the Salvage Shop in less than ten
minutes! We'd have done it in nine if it hadn't been
for that cross-wind on the prom.

STEPHEN I only hope I live to tell the tale.

SYLVIE I hope Nellie McGrath and her poodles do, too.
Them lights are still out on the prom, Katie. Nearly
bowled poor Nellie over, so we did, and scattered
the two poodles to the four winds.

KATIE They'll be glad to be liberated from that one.

EDDIE That's enough, Kate! (*Silence*) I thought you'd have
more sense, Rita — it's pitch-dark out there.

RITA (*Trying to conceal her enjoyment*) It was Sylvie's idea,
wasn't it, Sylvie? I only did what I was told.

SYLVIE Like the loyal lieutenant you are!

EDDIE The bloody chair could have turned over.

SYLVIE That's right. And we could have been struck by a
tidal wave on the prom, too — but we weren't.
Relax, Eddie! It was an epic journey, wasn't it, Rita?
And a fitting climax to a memorable night. Tabernacle, Stephen! Give that man a drink. Give us all a
drink. (KATIE *goes to parlour for glasses as* STEPHEN
gingerly approaches tabernacle) Don't worry, Stephen
— it's de-consecrated.

STEPHEN Just the one now, Sylvie.

SYLVIE (*As* KATIE *organises drinks, glasses etc. Mimics* STEPHEN)
'Just the one now, Sylvie'. You can be sure of it,

Stephen — one at a time! I didn't see you in the hall, Eddie.

EDDIE   I was there. (*Pause*) It was a good night, Sylvie.

STEPHEN   No more than the Captain deserved.

SYLVIE   I'm not so sure about that, Stephen, but we'll let it pass. (KATIE *gives him a drink*) To tell the truth, I was dreading the whole affair. The prospect of watching Reilly hang his conscience out to dry wasn't exactly enticing. Not to mention being wheeled up the aisle in this yoke so the good citizens of Garris could see how far gone I was. But you're right, Eddie, it *was* a good night. (*Raises glass*) I propose a toast. (*All but* EDDIE *raise their glasses*) To the Garristown Brass. To the colour of what *is*! (*Pause*) To *acceptance*. (*Pause. They all look at* EDDIE) Raise your glass, Eddie.

EDDIE   No.

SYLVIE   You have no choice. None of us has. Raise your glass!

EDDIE   No! I won't drink to that! You do if you want to, Sylvie, but I won't.

RITA   (*Quietly*) Raise your glass, Eddie. Sylvie's right. You have no choice.

Silence. He looks at them all — lastly to SYLVIE *in the chair. Then decides. Slugs back whiskey.*

EDDIE   There! To acceptance! Satisfied, Rita? (*Pours another drink*) And here's another one. To giving up! (*Drinks. Pours another*) And last but not least — to lying down and fucking dying! Okay now, Sylvie? Okay, everybody! (*Slams down the glass*) I have work to do. (*Crosses to work-bench*) Someone has to mind the shop, y'know. (*Some activity on timber with manual planer, the rhythm gradually increasing to a frenzy*) Can't all be ducking off. Can't all be going off fucking dying, y'know. Somebody has to stay in the shop. Lights on. Doors open. Ready for business in the Salvage Shop. The fucking Salvage Shop, hah! Only nothing to be salvaged anymore! (*Hurls the*

planer violently to one side. Collapses in tears on work-
bench, beating his fists violently against it). Don't go on
me, Sylvie! Don't go fucking dying on me! You can't go
yet!

KATIE Da! No, Da! It's all right. (*Grabs him. Embraces him*)
It's all right, Da. It's all right.

RITA We're all here, Eddie. We're all here, aren't we,
Stephen?

STEPHEN Be sure of it, Eddie. All here together.

EDDIE Sorry. I'm sorry. Tired, that's all. (*Gestures to heart*)
In here, y'know. I'm sorry, Sylvie. Just like old times.
Fucked it all up again, didn't I?

SYLVIE No, Eddie. You didn't. (*Pause*) Leave him now.
(*Nobody moves*) Leave him. He'll be safe with me.

STEPHEN C'mon, girls. I'll walk ye home.

KATIE No. I'm staying here.

EDDIE Go home, Kate.

KATIE This *is* my home. (*Collects bags. Goes to* SYLVIE.
Kisses him) I'll see you in the morning, Sylvie.

KATIE *goes out to parlour area.*

RITA Goodnight, Sylvie. (*Pause*) I love you, Eddie Tansey.
I know that's crossing the line. But what the hell?

RITA *leaves.*

STEPHEN (*To* EDDIE) They'll be around for the windows in the
morning. The unveiling's on Sunday, Sylvie — the
band have the shout for the ceremony. Y'might get
along if you're up to it.

SYLVIE I wouldn't miss it. Goodnight, Stephen. And
thanks.

STEPHEN It was my pleasure — Captain Tansey.

STEPHEN *exits. Silence.*

SYLVIE Here. (*Glass*) Put a drink in that.

EDDIE You've had enough.

SYLVIE I haven't even started.

EDDIE You're on tablets, remember.

SYLVIE Matter a damn now.

EDDIE (*Taking glass*) Just the one, so. It's late. Drink that and I'll give you a hand with them stairs.

SYLVIE It's only eleven o'clock. I'll be lying down long enough.

EDDIE I'll check on Katie, so.

SYLVIE Leave her, Eddie. Katie's all right. So am I. And I'm sure Nellie McGrath's poodles have turned up by now, too. Will you just take it easy for a minute? (*Pause*) I gather Mr Pavarotti regrets —

EDDIE It was on the cards. It doesn't matter.

SYLVIE It mattered to you. Thanks, Eddie. For what you were trying to do. If I wasn't so stubborn I would have said as much before. If I wasn't so bloody arrogant I would have had the decency to tell you the debt was all mine.

EDDIE None of it matters now.

SYLVIE Yes. It does. Because *you* have to get up in the morning and let the light in. You have to keep going, Eddie. So we have to get it straight and we're running out of time. I was the one who betrayed you. You know that, don't you?

EDDIE It doesn't matter.

SYLVIE You know it. And you need to hear me say it. Maybe I need to say it, too. All I saw was the empty chair. All I heard was the music. Those perfect notes all I ever cared about. I didn't give a damn why you'd gone missing. The music would heal that. I'd heal it through the music. I'd forgotten, of course. There is pain which no music can describe; there are conditions for which no music exists. I know that now, Eddie. I'm the one who's sorry.

EDDIE We have to let go of that now. The both of us.

SYLVIE We'll drink to that — one for the road! (*Sips whiskey*) For thirty-seven years, I pushed and bullied and browbeat that band towards a version of itself impossible to attain. I tried to take them past their limits. We had a sacred function in this place — Minister and Minstrel entwined — and by Christ we were going to live up to it. But tonight I sat in that hall and listened to the band and I fell in love with imperfection. The bum notes, the off keys, the shady timings — in my profound arrogance, I'd forgotten they had their function, too, and that it was a necessary and noble one. (*Pause*) Reilly invited me up, you know. Decent enough of the old bollox, I suppose, and churlish to refuse. I stood before them one last time and it was *good*, Eddie. It was a good feeling. Everything in harmony at last. And that's when I understood. The flawed note was sacred, too. When I turned to take a bow, I was looking for you. I wanted you to see that something had shifted. That Sylvie had found his peace at last — that you must find it, too. (*Pause*) Master Reilly offered his baton as a keepsake. Silver plated, too, if you don't mind. I thanked him but demurred. (*Takes baton from wheelchair*) I have my own, y'see. Bruised and battered like meself but if it could talk — (*Gets up from the chair. Crosses to* EDDIE) It was my father's before me. (*Offers baton to* EDDIE) It's yours now, *Maestro. Maestro Tansey.*

> KATIE *returns and watches as* EDDIE, *uncertain, looks at baton, then back to* SYLVIE. *Silence. He takes the baton, clasping* SYLVIE's *hand as he does. At the moment they touch, we hear 'Una furtiva lagrima'.* SYLVIE *begins to conduct, but the gesture is in the lower register — it is an indication to* EDDIE, *who now joins him, somewhat self-consciously at first, but with gradually increasing assurance. They look at one another. Then* SYLVIE *turns, crosses the stage and begins to climb the stairs, as* EDDIE *continues to conduct and the music soars and the lights fade to blackout.*